An opinionated guide to

LONDON NEIGHBOURHOODS

Written by
JAMES MANNING

Monmouth Street, Covent Garden (no.2)

INFORMATION IS DEAD. LONG LIVE OPINION.

When we conceived these guidebooks, we feared they would fail. Who needs a guidebook when everything can be googled for free?

But then it occurred to us: that's exactly why you *do* want a guidebook. You want lively, trustworthy opinion combined with great photographs. You don't want endless information from a thousand online bots.

We think you are like us: you care about quality, you care about style, you care about provenance, but you don't have time to waste on long words like 'provenance'. You want to cut to the chase: where's good?

If you were to come and stay on our couch (it's a metaphor btw; we have a guide to hotels), these are the places we'd recommend.

Ann & Martin, co-founders
Hoxton Mini Press

Granary Square, King's Cross (no.18)

Greenwich Park, Greenwich (no.34)

KEEP IT LOCAL

London isn't one place: it's hundreds. Zoom in on the brown blur of the metropolis and a constellation of villages and towns emerges – a city of neighbourhoods. Many started life as hamlets outside the medieval city of London. The city sprawled, throwing out new circles of housing and industry like rings on a tree trunk. London gobbled up the surrounding villages, while new districts sprouted from fields, forests and marsh. Eventually, it even absorbed whole towns like Greenwich (no.34), Walthamstow (no.30) and Richmond (no.14).

In this patchwork metropolis, there's a neighbourhood for everyone's taste: from historical to hip, leafy to louche, Georgian to Brutalist. If you ever feel tired of London (or indeed life), it's easy to switch things up and experience somewhere wholly new, without even straying off the Tube map. After all, this is perhaps the most diverse and exciting city on earth.

That diversity shouldn't be taken for granted. It's threatened by malicious political actors who cast London's multiculturalism as a weakness rather than its ultimate strength. But it's also at risk from the same market forces that have always shaped its development.

London is constantly changing. (By the time you read this book, many of the places in it will already have evolved or even disappeared.) Sometimes that's a good thing, creating opportunities and space for new ideas, new businesses and new Londoners. But gentrification and homogenisation are real threats to what makes the city great. Even well-meaning developers can end up breaking up communities, pricing out long-time residents and replacing independent, local businesses with stale chains.

It's tough for any neighbourhood to keep moving into the future while keeping hold of the things that make it special. But the best places in London will always save space for the old, the weird, the inexpensive and the defiantly un-shiny.

Of the hundreds of neighbourhoods in the city, this guide features 40 of my favourites. It goes big on the things that make me happy: bookshops, record shops, pubs and cocktail bars, affordable-but-amazing restaurants, great coffee, museums and art, gig venues, indie cinemas, street markets, delis and parks. And if I missed out *your* favourite part of the city, I can only apologise. Please email the publisher and they might go for a second edition.

James Manning
London, 2026

James Manning is an award-winning journalist and lifelong Londoner, who grew up in an SW postcode but now lives in E. He has spent the last 13 years covering the culture, food and nightlife of London (and beyond) for *Time Out*. He previously co-authored Hoxton Mini Press's *Opinionated Guide to London Bookshops*.

BEST FOR...

Cheap eats

It's hard to beat Chinatown (no.3) for sheer density of affordable restaurants, but Dalston (no.26) runs it close with its plentiful Turkish grills, and Brixton (no.35) and Peckham (no.37) serve up a whole world of global cuisines at very decent prices.

Top-drawer dinners

The food scenes in Highbury (no.20) and Clerkenwell (no.6) punch way above their weight, both hosting some of London's best restaurants. And Covent Garden (no.2) has some truly great options alongside the tourist traps and chains.

Art and museums

Get cultured in the City (no.4) at the Barbican and Guildhall Art Gallery; hit up Bloomsbury (no.5) for the epic British Museum and a clutch of smaller, stranger spaces; or drop in to Mayfair (no.7) for one of the world's greatest clusters of free-to-visit commercial galleries.

Big nights out

The post-industrial 'Bermondsey triangle' (no.36) is London's low-key nightlife hotspot right now – but there's always a gig or a party going on in Camden Town (no.16), and Soho (no.1) has provided legendary late nights for countless decades.

Indie shopping

Coal Drops Yard in King's Cross (no.18) has a sublime edit of retailers all in one place, while Notting Hill (no.10) is great for all things second-hand. There are high streets full of independent businesses in Stoke Newington (no.15) and Crouch End (no.17).

Countryside vibes

City life doing you down? You don't need to go much further for your fix of greenery than Richmond (no.14) with its deer-filled park and river walks; Hampstead (no.21) for its stately homes and wild swims; the leafy lanes of Dulwich (no.33); or Leytonstone (no.28) and Walthamstow (no.30), gateways to Epping Forest.

Marvellous markets

East London has no end of great markets, from flowers on Columbia Road (no.27) to street eats and crafty treats on Broadway Market (no.25). Or head west, where Chiswick (no.13) rotates between cheese, flower and food markets.

History hunting

The age of sail lives on in maritime Greenwich (no.34), while splendid Chelsea (no.11) and Kensington (no.9) wear their centuries of oligarchy well. Or visit the 18th century in Spitalfields (no.24), where you can step through centuries of history in a Huguenot townhouse.

SEASONAL EVENTS

CHINESE NEW YEAR

Falling between late January and mid-February, the Chinese (or Lunar) New Year begins with the second new moon following the winter solstice. London hosts one of the biggest celebrations outside Asia, and Chinatown is the epicentre, with a spectacular parade, lion dances to bring good luck, festive set menus and decorations that bring the Chinese zodiac to life.

Chinatown / January–February / lccauk.com

OXFORD VS CAMBRIDGE BOAT RACE

For over 150 years, the dark blues (Oxford) and the light blues (Cambridge) have sent their best rowers to race a 4.2-mile stretch of the Thames between Putney and Mortlake. Grab a pint and a spot along the Chiswick embankment to watch the final sprint, before settling in at a local pub afterparty.

Chiswick / March–April / theboatrace.org

LONDON MARATHON

One of the world's most iconic (and popular) marathons, the London Marathon starts in Blackheath and winds 26.2 miles through the capital to end on the Mall. Greenwich is a great place to cheer on runners, at mile 6 of the course. Whether you're watching the elites zip past or yelling encouragement at the thousands running for charity, it's a thoroughly inspiring day out.

Greenwich / April / londonmarathonevents.co.uk

Ever wanted to watch a herd of waiters charging through Soho's streets, balancing trays of champagne and glasses? The long-standing Waiters' Race is the culmination of Soho's charming 'village' fair, when the garden of St Anne's Church is packed with live music, drag and other free, quirky festivities.

Soho / July / thesohosociety.org.uk

NOTTING HILL CARNIVAL

A legendary fixture in London's calendar, August bank holiday sees Notting Hill transformed into a joyful celebration of Caribbean music, culture and food. Sunday is the family-friendly day, with the more raucous main parade on Monday.

Notting Hill / August / nhcarnival.org

FRIEZE SCULPTURE

Each autumn, Frieze Art Fair arrives in Regent's Park, filling two marquees with art and dotting sculptures by world-famous artists amid the greenery outside. The fairs are ticketed, but the outdoor sculpture display is free – and infinitely calmer.

Marylebone / September–November / frieze.com

THE LORD MAYOR'S SHOW

Since the 13th century, the Lord Mayor has made an annual journey from the City of London to Westminster to swear allegiance to the Crown. The free parade is a gloriously chaotic miscellany of floats, horses, dancers, marching bands and London lore.

City of London / November / lordmayorsshow.london

1
SOHO

Glitz, glamour and gaiety,
scrubbed up for modern times

Nowhere in London has accumulated more mythology per square foot than the grimy, glitzy grid of Soho. Once a cholera-afflicted slum home to poets, courtesans and seditionaries, then London's red-light district, and latterly the centre of LGBTQ+ life in the capital, Soho has retained its subversive reputation despite decades of gentrification. Yes, the tide of swanky restaurants and chains that washed away some of the sleaze has coincided with the closures of some Soho classics: Madame Jojo's, The Gay Hussar, the original Patisserie Valerie, Camisa's deli… And yes, *everyone* says Soho was better when they were young – whether that was in the 1960s or the 2010s. But there's still a feast of fun to be had along these storied streets, still a community of local characters to reward hours of people-watching, and still more than enough haunts – including some worthy newcomers – to ensure Soho stays London's essential late-night neighbourhood.

Soho Square

<u>DO</u>

From day to night, Soho always delivers. Start with a daytime wander around **Berwick Street Market** or see something thought-provoking at the **Sadie Coles HQ** or **The Photographers' Gallery**. After dinner, catch a comedy show at **Soho Theatre**, a film at the **Curzon Soho** or a jazz gig at **Ronnie Scott's** or the long-established **PizzaExpress Jazz Club**. Then hop the gay clubs and pubs along **Old Compton Street**, and crash out at **Hazlitt's**, a Victorian time warp of a boutique hotel.

<u>EAT</u>

Order modern European dishes from a handwritten menu at the candlelit **Andrew Edmunds**. Watch chefs cook up a Thai storm from a counter seat at **KILN**. Sample Cambodian food at **Mamapen** (permanent kitchen resident at The Sun & 13 Cantons pub) or go Sri Lankan at **Paradise** or the original **Hoppers**. Pair fried chicken with cocktails and natural wine at **Rita's**. Pretend you're in Paris at the swish **Brasserie Zédel** or **L'Escargot**, soon to celebrate 100 years serving French classics on Greek Street. And for something sweet? Visit **Maison Bertaux** (established 1871) for creamy patisserie, **Panadera** for Filipino pastries or **Gelupo** for offbeat ice-cream flavours like watermelon sorbet or ricotta sour cherry.

<u>DRINK</u>

The classic Soho watering holes are **The French House**, where beer comes only in half pints (you can also dine in style upstairs), and **The Coach & Horses** on Greek Street, formerly and famously home to London's

Bar Italia

grumpiest landlord. Meanwhile, **Trisha's** (alias the New Evaristo Club) is a speakeasy-style basement bar that's hosted many a raucous late one.

SHOP

Scoop up rare books at **IDEA** and titles of all kinds at the behemoth that is **Foyles**. Browse an astonishing range of magazines at **Good News**. Stock up on beans (or grab a bargain cup o' joe) at **Algerian Coffee Stores**, keeping Soho awake since 1887. Hit the record stores around **Berwick Street** and **Broadwick Street**. Style up your life at the **Alex Eagle** or **Earl of East** concept stores, and shop second-hand gems at **Reign Vintage**, **Dukes Cupboard** and **Beyond Retro**.

Above: Algerian Coffee Stores
Opposite: Andrew Edmunds

2

COVENT GARDEN

Touristy but somehow underrated: a West End gem

A bustling, colourful chunk of the West End, Covent Garden is probably best known for its former flower market (as depicted in *My Fair Lady*). Now converted into a shopping mall and pedestrianised 'piazza', it's big on architectural charm but often swerved by Londoners on account of the throngs of tourists and street entertainers. (The Tube station is also famous as one of London's most unpleasant and difficult to escape.) But dismiss Covent Garden at your peril. Despite the hordes, it remains among central London's greatest neighbourhoods for culture, eating, drinking, indie shopping and atmospheric strolls – especially around the historic micro-neighbourhood of Seven Dials.

Covent Garden Market

Covent Garden Market

MARKET

DO

West End theatres and the **Royal Ballet and Opera** dominate the cultural landscape, but dig deeper to find **The Garden Cinema** and the ironically named **Top Secret Comedy Club**. **London Transport Museum** is fascinating, and nearby **Somerset House** and the **Courtauld Gallery** host brilliant exhibitions of art old and new.

EAT

Dodge the tourist traps with no-frills Asian flavours: Japanese at **Eat Tokyo**, **Kangnam Pocha** for Korean, **Banh Mi Aha!** for Vietnamese, or Chinese at **Lanzhou Lamian**. For something fancier, grab one of the 24 counter seats at **The Barbary**, dig into British seafood classics at **Parsons** or sample the Anglo-Indian fusion dishes of **Tandoor Chop House**.

DRINK

Your eclectic bar crawl could take in classy cocktail joints like **Oriole** and **Freud**, old-school French wine bar **Le Beaujolais**, West End haven the **Phoenix Arts Club**, **Club Soda** (for sober drinkers) and dive bar **BLOODsports**, which screens football games and horror movies.

SHOP

Pick up vintage clothes at **Rokit**. Buy a bag of beans at **Monmouth Coffee Company**. Sniff some natural toiletries at the original **Neal's Yard Remedies** or go HAM on cheese at **Neal's Yard Dairy**. And for bibliophiles, **Cecil Court** is possibly the greatest street in London, lined with a fabulous array of independent booksellers.

Cecil Court

3

CHINATOWN

London's home of Chinese culture (and food)

Sandwiched between the swish of Soho and the picture palaces and tourist traps of Leicester Square, this tiny neighbourhood was not London's original Chinatown. (That was founded in the Limehouse docks in the 1880s, and lasted for nearly a century.) Nor is it London's only real Chinatown today: there are expanding clusters of Chinese businesses in Bloomsbury (no.5) and in Holborn, Aldgate and the Isle of Dogs. Still, Chinatown has been the symbolic home of London's Chinese community since the 1970s, and it's been revitalised of late by a new wave of arrivals from Hong Kong – and a newfound fame on TikTok. Gerrard Street and Lisle Street are hung year-round with thousands of red-and-yellow lanterns, Newport Place is thick with tables for alfresco dining and the Chinatown Gate on Wardour Street is a popular spot for selfies. There's even an incipient Koreatown springing up next door, on Charing Cross Road.

DO

This is the spiritual home of British cinema. Catch a block-buster at one of the Leicester Square theatres or a midnight movie at the legendary **Prince Charles Cinema**. And pay homage to film director Jean Cocteau, whose murals adorn the church of **Notre Dame de France**.

EAT

Dim sum, of course: there are more than 100 restaurants crammed into these streets, most specialising in Cantonese cuisine. Load the table with steamed goodies at **Leong's Legend**, **Golden Phoenix** or **Wong Kei**, a stalwart with famously brusque service. **C&R Cafe Restaurant** and **Rasa Sayang** serve incredible plates of Malaysian rice and noodles, **Chinese Tapas House** doles out bargain-basement egg crepes loaded with crispy tofu and sweet, spicy sauce, and **Newport Court** – alias 'Dessert Alley' – is the place to go for matcha soft serve, takoyaki and more sweet stuff from across East Asia.

DRINK

Happy Lemon and **Kova Patisserie** are good bets for bubble tea. **The Blue Posts** is a trendy but traditional pub and Dutch haven **De Hems** serves dozens of beers from the Low Countries – with bitterballen on the side.

SHOP

Stock up on pan-Asian groceries at **SeeWoo**, **Loon Fung** and **Xin Long Men**. Or duck down an alleyway to **Lo's Noodle Factory**, where you can pick up bundles of ho fun and cheung fun noodles straight from the source.

Chinatown Gate, Wardour Street

4

THE CITY

The historic square mile

Is there anything to the City of London but funny-shaped glass towers full of money? Of course there is – though there's certainly a *lot* of money here. As well as being Britain's financial powerhouse for the last several centuries, the City is a peculiarly medieval place. Its street pattern goes back a thousand years, but most of its buildings are either high-tech office blocks or grand Edwardian stone affairs. It's run by an arcane 'corporation' instead of a regular council, is guarded not only by its own police force but also by a series of metal dragons on its boundaries and a 'ring of steel' dating back to the era of IRA bombings, and is populated almost entirely by people who don't live here – the financial-sector workers who pour in every weekday as they have since the invention of the railways, hybrid working be damned. Visit on the weekend to dodge the suits and explore this fascinating square mile at its quietest.

St Paul's Cathedral

DO

Despite the City being repeatedly destroyed over the centuries, there's a tonne of history to see here. Delve into Roman foundations at the **London Mithraeum** and **Guildhall Art Gallery**. Tour the **Tower of London**, the capital's medieval fortress and royal prison. Climb the 311 steps of the pillar-like **Monument to the Great Fire of London**. Visit any of the dozens of city churches, many rebuilt after the fire by Christopher Wren, and explore his masterpiece: the magnificence of **St Paul's Cathedral**. Get lost in the sprawling **Barbican**, a Brutalist masterpiece of flats, gardens, courtyards, lobbies and arts venues – plus the spectacular **Barbican Conservatory** – that replaced areas bombed to bits during World War II. (**St Dunstan in the East Church Garden** is another unusual green oasis.) And look out on the modern face of the City from the free viewing platforms at **Sky Garden**, **Horizon 22** or **The Lookout**.

EAT

The office workers might survive mostly on sandwiches and salads, but you don't have to. Bloomberg Arcade is home to a whole row of decent restaurants, from curries at **Brigadiers** to udon at **Koya**. Nearby **Sweetings** has been serving fish lunches since the reign of Queen Victoria. For something much more recent, head to **BOXHALL**: a food court in a refurbished Edwardian arcade near Liverpool Street station.

Leadenhall Market

DRINK

All that financial machination calls for plenty of caffeine, and **Rosslyn Coffee** serves up the good stuff at its six outposts across the City. If you've got time to linger, the City does a nice line in ecclesiastical-flavoured cafes: **Host**, **Café Below** and **The Wren** all serve a nice cuppa in spectacular church settings. For a pint, nip down Bush Lane to the cosy **Bell** or try to nab one of the handful of riverside tables at **The Banker**. Or have a glass of vino at stylish **Fox**, a converted umbrella shop.

SHOP

This isn't the place to shop till you drop unless you're on a banker's budget, but **The Royal Exchange** is worth a wander, with luxury brands in a spectacular neoclassical building. Another soaring Victorian landmark, **Leadenhall Market**, is home to purveyors of all the little essentials: cheese, wine, flowers and cigars.

Above: Fox Fine Wines & Spirits
Below: metal dragon marking the boundary of the City

5

BLOOMSBURY

The capital's most clever-clogs neighbourhood

Brainy and bookish, Bloomsbury is studded with intellectual and cultural powerhouses. The British Museum, one of the world's biggest and oldest, leads a pack of smaller and more offbeat museums and galleries. University College London is the largest of a whole range of academic institutions occupying Bloomsbury's storied streets and squares. Bookshops aplenty cater to scholastic, radical and even occult tastes. And, of course, there's a local heritage of artists, scholars and writers that takes in everyone from Charles Dickens to Charles Darwin – plus the 1920s Bloomsbury Group, who were as famous for their sexual escapades as they were for pushing the boundaries of literature and economics. And if all that intellectual stuff makes you hungry, Bloomsbury's restaurant, cafe and bakery scene means there's plenty to nourish your belly as well as your brain.

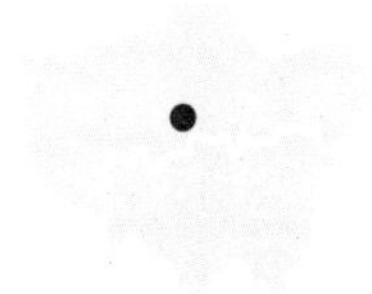

DO

Hit the museums! As well as the endless loot at **The British Museum**, you can ogle pickled animals at the **Grant Museum**, medical exhibits at the **Wellcome Collection**, a wealth of Dickens paraphernalia at his former home, the **Charles Dickens Museum**, and heartfelt 'identifying' objects left by mothers with their babies at the **Foundling Museum**, once a hospital for abandoned children.

EAT

From okonomiyaki at **Abeno** to Xi'an noodles at **Master Wei** and kimchi rice at **Seoul Bakery**, this area of London is great for Asian eats. There's also superb Levantine cooking at **Honey & Co.** and old-school Italian at **Ciao Bella**. If you're here before 11am, join the queue for beignets (doughnut-style pastries) from **Fortitude Bakehouse**.

DRINK

For coffee, hit up swish **Store Street Espresso** or welcoming corner spot **Knockbox**. For a pint, choose between **The Lamb**, with its Victorian 'snob screens' or the backstreet **Duke**, a time warp to the 1930s (apart from the price of booze). And for vino, you won't find better than **Noble Rot**, home to the eponymous magazine.

SHOP

Books, books, books – second-hand bargains from **Skoob** and **Judd**, mystical tomes from **Treadwell's**, radical manifestos from **Bookmarks** and keenly curated new reads from **London Review Bookshop** (and pop into **Present & Correct** next door for stylish stationery).

Above: The British Museum; Fortitude Bakehouse
Below: Judd Books; The British Library

6

CLERKENWELL

A magical corner of tucked-away central London

If a genie offered to conjure you up a flat anywhere in central London, Clerkenwell would be a strong contender. It's close to the West and East End action and chock-full of great stuff to eat, drink and do, but it's also surprisingly tranquil and residential – at least beyond the main roads. If all you do is chug along Rosebery Avenue on a double-decker, you won't see most of what makes Clerkenwell great: corner pubs and Victorian lanes, pocket-sized green spaces and little rows of shops hosting all sorts of independent retailers – plus a mix of housing that takes in everything from grand squares and flipped warehouses to pioneering council estates. It all adds up to somewhere with more of a sense of community, and fewer bland chain shops, than you'll find almost anywhere else in Zone 1. Now, about that genie…

●

rown
Tavern

DO

Visit **The Postal Museum** and ride the Mail Rail: an underground railway that carried letters across London for 76 years. Catch a dance performance at **Sadler's Wells** theatre. Dig into local history at **The London Archives** and **Islington Museum**. Catch a B-movie at the tiny (35 seats!) **Nickel** cinema. And from 2026, you'll also be able to visit the **Quentin Blake Centre for Illustration**.

EAT

In the '90s, Clerkenwell invented the gastropub and 'nose-to-tail' eating, at **The Eagle** and **St. John** respectively (both still going strong). More recently, **Sessions Arts Club** and the revived **Quality Chop House** have kept that British fine-dining legacy alive. For everyday eats, stroll down **Exmouth Market – Morito, Shawarma Bar** and **Morchella** make it feel almost Mediterranean.

DRINK

Clerkenwell excels at low-key backstreet pubs. **The Sekforde** is an upmarket standout, with its wood-panelled bar and famous Sunday roast, while the tiny **Harlequin** has a dinky, leafy beer garden.

SHOP

Exmouth Cultural Kiosk sells books and pamphlets from an old news kiosk, while **magCulture** stocks an incredible array of magazines. **Clerkenwell's Coffee & Books** is another great stop for reading matter. And you can shop for offbeat prints from satirical artist **Mr Bingo** at his Amwell Street shop/studio, open Fridays only.

Above: magCulture; Smithfield Market
Below: Sessions Arts Club; St. John

Exmouth Market

EXMOUTH
MARKET E.C.1

7

MAYFAIR &
ST JAMES'S

A dazzling display of art, architecture and wealth

Mayfair has been a plutocrat's playground since it was first founded in the 18th century. Walk through it today, and you'll pass high-end tailors, red-brick mansion blocks (and full-blown mansions), five-star hotels with top-hatted doormen, umpteen blue plaques, auction houses, designer boutiques and discreet offices – everything that could possibly be needed for servicing the international superelite. St James's, on the other side of Piccadilly, is less flashy and more old-money, but still geared to the ultrarich. And what about the rest of us? Well, you don't *have* to be a fat cat to have a good time around here (though it undeniably helps). It's always fun to wander the glitzy streets and cobbled mews, pop into a gallery or three and catch a glimpse of how the 0.1 per cent live.

The Audley Public House

<u>DO</u>

Mayfair is the perfect place to catch free art – or rather, very expensive art that you don't have to pay a penny to see. Roam the **Cork Street** commercial galleries plus **Gagosian, Sadie Coles, Shapero Modern** and **White Cube Mason's Yard. The Royal Academy**'s exhibitions are mostly *not* free, but often great. Tour the homes of two musical maestros: GF Handel and Jimi Hendrix, who lived in neighbouring Brook Street houses a couple of centuries apart (now the **Handel Hendrix House**).

<u>EAT</u>

Skip the glitzy restaurants serving adequate food at oligarch prices and explore **Shepherd Market** or **Heddon Street** for better, more affordable cooking. Or grab a pizza at **Mercato Mayfair**, a deconsecrated church improbably converted into a bustling food hall.

<u>DRINK</u>

Everyone should try a martini from the trolley at **DUKES** at least once in their life – but for everyday drinking, head for the refreshingly old-school **The Red Lion** in St James or the gorgeous, art-bedecked **Audley** in Mayfair.

<u>SHOP</u>

Assuming you aren't looking to drop a grand, stick to Piccadilly's affordable-yet-fancy mainstays like **Fortnum & Mason, Hatchards** and Europe's biggest bookshop, the flagship **Waterstones**. Nearby **Jermyn Street** and **St James's Street** are worth a gander for traditional shops selling menswear, cigars, cheese, wine and, er, guns.

Claridge's

FORTNUM & MASON

Above: Sadie Coles; Below: The Audley Public House
Opposite: Fortnum & Mason

8

MARYLEBONE

Swanky but welcoming corner of Zone 1

There are two types of tourists in Marylebone. The first elbow their way to Madame Tussauds and the Sherlock Holmes Museum, at the great detective's actual (fictional) address on Baker Street. The second makes surreptitious tracks to Harley Street, which is lined with swanky medical clinics. But there's plenty more to Marylebone than waxworks and nose jobs. With its smart mansion blocks, garden squares and well-to-do high street, this neighbourhood is surprisingly village-like for somewhere within spitting distance of Oxford Street. A tidy Georgian grid intersected by the meander of Marylebone Lane – which follows the submerged River Tyburn – it's also connected to the underrated Lisson Grove area and the lawns and gardens of Regent's Park. There's a plethora of cultural and culinary options, and even some decent nightlife, if you know where to look. And of course, no end of shopping opportunities – whether or not you've got money to burn at Selfridges.

DO

Catch a classic film at **Regent Street Cinema**, the UK's oldest picture house. Browse paintings by Rubens, Rembrandt and Velázquez at the **Wallace Collection**, get up-to-date at contemporary galleries **Arcadia Missa** and the **Lisson Gallery** or see something quirky at the tiny **Gallery of Everything**.

EAT

Go high-end at Michelin-starred **AngloThai** or OTT Austrian grand cafe **Fischer's**. Or go low at the cheerfully grungy **Tommi's Burger Joint**, old-school sandwich emporium **Paul Rothe & Son** or two of London's greatest fish-and-chip shops: the **Golden Hind** and the **Seashell of Lisson Grove**.

DRINK

Props to **The Social, The Phoenix** and **The Albany**: three drinking dens that also double as gig and club venues, doing great work to keep fun alive in central London.

SHOP

Head to Chiltern Street for a deep dive into magazines at **Shreeji Newsagents**, whisky at **Cadenhead's** and Japanese ironmongery at **Niwaki**. Marylebone High Street has **Daunt Books**: a globetrotting temple to literature, with titles arranged by country. Master cutler **David Mellor** is nearby, as is the weekly **Marylebone Farmers' Market**. And up in Lisson Grove, **Alfies Antique Market** fills an entire block with indoor stalls selling pre-loved treasures.

Above: Paul Rothe & Son; Daunt Books
Below: Alfies Antique Market; Marylebone Farmers' Market

9

KENSINGTON

Culture aplenty in the home of London's elites

London's streets are famously *not* paved with gold – but if they were, the gilding would start here. This has been royal territory for centuries, with Kensington Palace and its gardens at its centre. Queen Victoria left the neighbourhood an especially grandiose legacy: the cultural quarter of South Kensington, with its museums, colleges, institutes and vast Royal Albert Hall. Turn left at the Albert Memorial, and you'll reach Kensington High Street, a string of chains that used to be a lot more interesting: Kensington Market and Biba drew fashionistas here for decades. Beyond that are terraces of townhouses, garden squares, private schools, embassies and posh restaurants. There's a bit more diversity around Kensington's edges, like the cluster of Middle Eastern businesses around Gloucester Road Tube and the remnants of a Polish expat community dating back to World War II. But really, most people visit the area these days for high culture – and Kensington's got it in spades.

•

The Royal Albert Hall

DO

Tour the museums: the enormous **V&A**, with its beautiful Victorian cafe, and the kid-friendly **Natural History** and **Science Museums**. Don't skip the **Design Museum** for fascinating exhibitions in a spectacular building, and the ornate **Leighton House** and **Sambourne House**, former homes of the painter and cartoonist, respectively. Afterwards, stroll through **Holland Park** and spot the resident peacocks – or catch a French movie at **Ciné Lumière**, part of the Institut Français.

EAT

It's hard to dodge the chains around here, especially on a budget. But you can dine in fine Polish style at **Ognisko** or, for something more affordable, go Lebanese at **Baba Ghanouj** (near Gloucester Road) or plant-based at **Mali Vegan Thai** (near Earl's Court). Scandi bakery **HJEM** and **The De Morgan** at Leighton House are lovely cafes.

DRINK

Have a glass at the cosy **Troubadour**, a live music club that's hosted plenty of greats – or head to **The Churchill Arms**, a famous spot bedecked in flowers or Christmas trees, depending on the season.

SHOP

The **Divertimenti** cookware shop sells gorgeous Italian ceramics as well as useful kitchen tools. Kensington's charity shops are (unsurprisingly) full of pre-loved designer bits at decent prices – or you could let the experts at **GOOD** boutique do the sifting for you.

Above: The V&A; Leighton House
Below: The Design Museum; The Churchill Arms

10
NOTTING HILL

Caribbean culture meets the boho jet set

Notting Hill is a legendary neighbourhood where multiple identities overlap. For most of the 20th century, it was a notorious slum whose cheap rents attracted immigrant communities, artists, squatters, punks and revolutionaries. The tense racial politics that gave rise to violent riots in the '50s also paradoxically birthed the raucously multicultural annual celebrations of Notting Hill Carnival. Carnival is a Caribbean thing, but you can spot the legacies of plenty more immigrant communities here: Iberian, North African, Serbian... Nevertheless, that's not what most people think of when they hear 'Notting Hill'. These days (partly thanks to romcom king Richard Curtis), the area's reputation is as a bourgeois-bohemian heartland, whose residents would rather flee to the Cotswolds or the Cayman Islands than embrace the chaos of Carnival. But you don't have to have a trust fund or a pair of boat shoes to dabble in Notting Hill's buzzy restaurant scene, queue for a viral pastry or play a game of 'spot the celeb'.

<u>DO</u>

Take a trip through a century of consumer culture at the eccentric **Museum of Brands**; catch a movie at the plush **Electric Cinema** or the historic **Gate Picturehouse**; stay up late at **Notting Hill Arts Club** or the low-key **Globe** nightclub; catch cultural happenings at **The Tabernacle** arts space; or take a guided tour of postmodernist masterpiece **The Cosmic House**. And of course, come for **Carnival** (as Londoners call it), when the area's streets are filled with blaring music, packed crowds and good times every August bank holiday – long may it continue.

<u>EAT</u>

Where to start? Prolific restaurateur Chris D'Sylva runs a clutch of famous-people favourites here, including **Dorian** and **Eel Sushi**. Jackson Boxer's **Dove** is a Modern British gem. Brunch is huge here – try **Granger & Co.** or **Beam** – as are gastropubs like **The Cow**, **The Pelican** and **The Fat Badger**. And there are global flavours too: eat Sicilian at **Panella**, Ukrainian at **Sino**, Nikkei (Japanese-Peruvian) at **FAN** or Thai at **Speedboat Bar**.

<u>DRINK</u>

It's always cocktail time in Notting Hill, so imbibe at tiki heaven **Trailer Happiness**, Dishoom's Bombay fantasy **Permit Room** or hard-partying go-to **Gold**. If you'd rather a pub without the gastro, then take a tip from punk icon Joe Strummer and order a pint at a more down-to-earth boozer, **The Elgin**.

Above: The Pelican; Books for Cooks
Below: typical Notting Hill mews house; Dorian

Buying stuff is a key reason to visit the neighbourhood – and a lot of that stuff is second-hand. Notting Hill is a hub for shops selling everything pre-loved, from clothes to vinyl, comics, furniture and even recipe books (at **Books for Cooks**). The main action is on **Portobello Road Market**, where hundreds of shops and stalls pop up to sell antiques, vintage clothes (from designer to bargain-basement) and tonnes more. The pros visit on Fridays, when it's quieter than weekends. Once you're done shopping, refuel with treats from cult bakeries, **Layla** or **Kuro**. And don't forget to pick up a pastel de nata from old-school Portuguese joints, **Lisboa** or **Oporto Patisserie**, and nose around Spanish delis, **R Garcia and Sons** and **La Plaza**: institutions that are still community hubs for the area's Iberian residents.

Notting Hill Carnival

11

CHELSEA

*High-net-worth enclave with
a surprisingly radical heritage*

Historic, tremendously wealthy and with a front-row view of central London's most splendid stretch of the Thames, Chelsea doesn't exactly seem like a cradle of sedition. But it's been home to more than its fair share of revolutionaries over the years, from Jonathan Swift to Oscar Wilde, Sylvia Pankhurst and most of the Rolling Stones. It played a key part in the rise of punk, with Malcolm McLaren and Vivienne Westwood opening their shop Sex on the King's Road in the '70s. True, that rebellious spirit seems pretty distant today. Chelsea is synonymous with the international superrich. You'll still spot the old-money Sloane Rangers of the '80s round here, and even a few old-school eccentrics, but Chelsea's lavish restaurants and shiny boutiques rival those of Mayfair (no.7) or Knightsbridge as venues for the world's upper crust to drop a couple of grand. Even so, this is London, and that means there's always something interesting to discover.

Sloane Square

DO

If you're not here for the annual **Chelsea Flower Show**, you can still get horticultural on a tour of the 350-year-old **Chelsea Physic Garden**. The **Saatchi Gallery** hosts decent exhibitions and the **606 Club** is a refreshingly down-to-earth spot for cosy jazz gigs. The experimental **Royal Court** theatre and classical concert venue **Cadogan Hall** add to Chelsea's cultural scene.

EAT

Sorry, you've come to the wrong place for cheap eats. If you do have cash to splash, try upscale Indian place **Kutir** – in an old townhouse – or Lyon-inspired bistro **Josephine**, from Michelin-acclaimed Claude Bosi. For those without expense accounts or trust funds, look in at **The Jam** – an eccentric Italian joint where half the tables are reached via ladders – and **Alley Cats Pizza**.

DRINK

Sink a pint by the fire at the **Fox & Hounds** or, for something completely different, sip a glass of natural wine at King's Road listening bar **New Forms**.

SHOP

Pavilion Road is a go-to for posh groceries, plus lovely books and stationery from **Papersmiths** and top-class kitchenware from **David Mellor**. There's a food market on **Duke of York Square** every Saturday, Italian goodies at **Luigi's** and **Prezzemolo & Vitale** and deli delights at **Arthur's Market**. **John Sandoe** is a must-visit bookshop and **BookBar** recently opened a Chelsea offshoot too.

Above: Chelsea Physic Garden; John Sandoe
Below: Duke of York Square Fine Food Market; the Saatchi Gallery

12

QUEEN'S PARK

An underrated chunk of west London

A mile and a half from the teeming streets of Notting Hill (no.10), Queen's Park is a far more laid-back slice of west London life. The area has a strong local identity, with a vocal residents' association, the only parish council in London and an annual Queen's Park Day and book festival. There's a huge and largely residential chunk south of the Tube, but if you're visiting, the action is north of the railway bridge. That's where you'll find the main drag of Salusbury Road – lined with cafes, pubs and handy shops – as well as Lonsdale Road: a mews where old workshops are now home to restaurants, bars and cafes (plus useful stuff like health clinics and coworking). On Sundays, the Queen's Park Farmers' Market spills out onto the mews and the hip crowd sports as many Trader Joe's tote bags as you'll see in any corner of Hackney. Nearby is Queen's Park itself, which pulls crowds with its lawns, cafe, dinky children's farm and woodland walk.

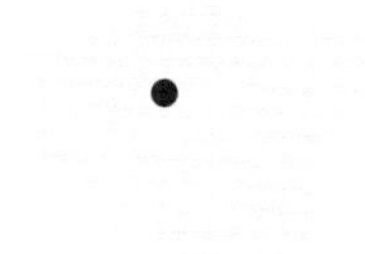

Wolfpack

DO

Into golf? Ruin a good walk with a game of pitch and putt in the eponymous park or work on your swing with a virtual driving session at **Tempo Golf Club**.

EAT

Flatbreads and small plates at **Carmel**, modern European delights at **Don't Tell Dad** or Aussie brunch at **Milk Beach** – all a few steps apart on Lonsdale Road. Twin gastropubs, **The Salusbury** and **Alice House**, anchor Salusbury Road. And don't miss **Michiko Sushino**, the sushi restaurant opened by fashion legend Michiko Koshino.

DRINK

Wolfpack serves beers from the west London craft brewery (owned by two former rugby pros) in a vibey, brick-walled taproom. **The Salusbury Winestore** is a cosy spot for a glass or two, plus a bottle to take home. And you can grab a Malaysian coffee to go (as well as a bite to eat) at **Sudu**, which even has a basement speakeasy.

SHOP

Stock up on reads at **Queen's Park Books**, a family-owned shop with a knowledgeable team. Sniff some nice-smelling natural toiletries at **Wilder Botanics**. And check if the eclectic **Brondesbury Flea Market** is on – it's well worth a visit if so.

Don't Tell Dad

13

CHISWICK

Go west for chi-chi shopping – and a few surprises

Running along the Thames and the old Roman road out of the city, Chiswick is a thoroughly pleasant chunk of west London. Eighteenth-century bigwigs like William Hogarth and Lord Burlington built country piles and riverside townhouses here to escape the Big Smoke; the Victorians added smart red-brick terraces and the Tube. Plentiful green spaces and Thames strolls – plus some solid options for eating, drinking and shopping – have sealed the deal: Chiswick is now a magnet for well-heeled London commuters. The action starts on the western fringes of Hammersmith and stretches all the way to Kew Bridge, with all sorts of micro-neighbourhoods along the way down Chiswick High Road. You'll also find an eccentric artist's house, a gin distillery, a very old brewery, an indie cinema and even a mini Soho House. Will you ever live here? Probably not (unless you already do – in which case, congrats!). But it's well worth the Tube ride out west.

DO

Tour the spectacular **Chiswick House**, whose splendid gardens are free to visit, and the home of pioneering designer **Emery Walker**. Go for a gin tasting at the **Sipsmith** distillery or a beer tour at the historic **Fuller's** brewery. Then gawp at the eye-popping **Mosaic House**, home to artist Carrie Reichardt. Whoever said Chiswick was boring?

EAT

If you're not here for the Michelin-starred **La Trompette**, check out the cafe scene around Turnham Green Tube instead – **Chief** even has a Japanese arcade upstairs. Meanwhile, unassuming **Napoli on the Road** has been named Europe's best pizzeria outside Italy – not once, but twice.

DRINK

If you're in search of lovely riverside pubs, picturesque Strand-on-the-Green has three: **The Bell & Crown**, **The City Barge** and **The Bull's Head**. Inland, try the Victorian gastropub **The Duke of Sussex** or **The George IV** – also home to **Headliners Comedy Club**.

SHOP

Old Market Place lives up to its name with rotating markets selling flowers, cheese and antiques. Duck down Devonshire Road for fine fish from **The Whistling Oyster**. And then go on a bookshop crawl, from old-school antiquarian **Foster Books** to **Bookcase, Everybody Reads** and **The Small Library Company**.

Above: The City Barge; Chiswick Flower Market
Below: Chiswick House

14

RICHMOND

Riverside strolls and acres of green

Richmond sits resplendent on the bank of the Thames: a vision of affluent suburbia. The river is a big part of life here: there's lots of messing about in boats, the waterfront is packed with restaurants, and tidal surges sometimes threaten the expensive shoes of unwary locals. Richmond has always been posh. The town grew up around the (now-vanished) Richmond Palace and royals bequeathed two epic parks to the populace: Richmond Park, with its acres of deer-dotted heathland, and the botanic wonderland of Kew Gardens. Georgian and Victorian bigwigs built grand townhouses, and the (now chain-choked) high street is punctuated by alleys of olde-worlde shops, pubs and cafes – several of which star in the series *Ted Lasso*, featuring the fictional AFC Richmond football team. There are two cinemas, at least two theatres, an outdoor swimming pool, unbelievable greenery and stellar views from the top of Richmond Hill. Just don't look too hard at the house prices.

Richmond Park

DO

Ramble through **Richmond Park** and **Kew Gardens** and walk the scenic towpath – or hire a rowing boat and cruise down to **Ham House** and back. Get cultured at **Richmond Theatre**, the **Orange Tree Theatre** or aboard the **Puppet Theatre Barge** (moored here seasonally). And take an alfresco dip at the (heated) **Pools on the Park**.

EAT

Petersham Nurseries, with its greenhouse restaurant and cafe, draws day-tripping foodies from all over. More humble but equally verdant is the **Hollyhock Cafe**, housed in a lovely chalet in Terrace Gardens. Alternatively, **Via Romana Deli** serves up legendary Italian sandwiches – follow it up with a cone from **Gelateria Danieli**.

DRINK

Bucolic boozing spots abound: **The Prince's Head** and **The Cricketers** are right on Richmond Green, while the **White Cross** is so close to the river that it regularly floods (wellies provided for those caught out).

SHOP

Browse books, flowers and knick-knacks along **Hill Rise**; vintage comics at **Raygun**; kids' books at **The Alligator's Mouth** or grown-up reads at **The Open Book**; kitchenware at **Kooks Unlimited**; gentlemen's apparel at **Heroes of Richmond** and **Curated Man**; or womenswear at **Margaret Howell**.

Petersham Nurseries

15

STOKE NEWINGTON

Hackney's chic and laid-back urban village

Straddling the border between north and east London and known simply as Stokey, this residential pocket has a village atmosphere. The spire of St Mary's Church towers over the rolling lawns and resident deer of Clissold Park. Traffic-free Stoke Newington Church Street is lined with indie shops. The Victorian backstreets, their terraced houses done up in waves since the '80s, are dotted with cute pubs and cafes. There's even a nearby wood: Abney Park, a cemetery and arboretum turned overgrown paradise for dog-walkers. But this is still London, and Stokey residents also have the useful shops, cocktail bars and the Turkish and Caribbean restaurants of Stoke Newington High Street and Green Lanes on their doorsteps – plus a smattering of stores serving the Charedi Jewish community in neighbouring Stamford Hill. It all makes for a neighbourhood that's more diverse and intriguing than meets the eye.

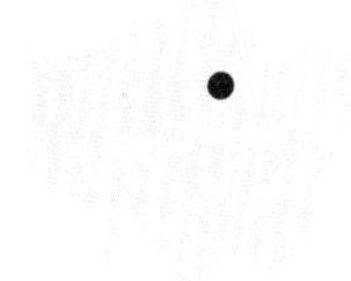

Clissold Park

DO

Take a dip: the **West Reservoir Centre** is a hub for outdoor swimming, as well as sailing and canoeing, under huge skies. Then warm up with a coffee and pastel de nata from the excellent Portuguese cafe on-site.

EAT

Rasa is a local classic, serving vegetarian Keralan food on Church Street since the '90s. **The Good Egg** dishes out delicious pitas; **Roti Spot** (formerly Roti Stop) is the go-to for Trinidadian takeaway; **Sonora Taquería** draws queues for its affordable tacos; and family-friendly **Cafe Z** is great for a Turkish breakfast. For something sweet, **Romeo & Giulietta** is a gem of a gelateria. Or tour the backstreet cafes for coffee and cake, stopping at brunch hub **Esters** or social enterprise **Luminary Bakery**.

DRINK

You'll wish **The Prince** could be your local, while the **White Hart** has a huge beer garden and **The Auld Shillelagh** is a contender for London's best Guinness pour. Or there's **Loading Bar**, where you can play classic arcade games while you drink.

SHOP

Bibliophiles should head to **Abney Books, Stoke Newington Bookshop** and **Church Street Bookshop**, and homebodies will find everything from kitchen gadgets to candles and throws at **Search & Rescue, Nook, Kitchen Provisions** and **Prep**. On the weekend, hit up the friendly **Growing Communities** farmers' market.

Above: Clissold Park; Growing Communities Market
Below: Search & Rescue; Esters

West Reservoir Centre

16

CAMDEN TOWN

Rock 'n' roll stomping ground and tourist nirvana

The counterculture still reigns in Camden... sort of. For decades, this bit of north London (and specifically Camden Market – a massive warren of yards and arches, packed with shops and stalls) has been a magnet for punks, goths, emo kids and other alternative types from all over the world. In truth, Camden today isn't somewhere many Londoners would choose to visit. But that's a bit unfair: this is still the best area in London to try on cheap silver jewellery, light-up rave clothes or bovver boots – and the people-watching is fantastic. Camden's live music legacy is still kicking, too: major artists by the spadeful played formative gigs around here (The Clash even shot their debut album cover in the market), and you'll catch both past and future legends at venues large and small, lining the musical mile from Mornington Crescent to Chalk Farm.

Camden Lock

DO

See a gig, obvs! Between the **Electric Ballroom**, the **Roundhouse**, **KOKO**, **The Dublin Castle**, **The Jazz Cafe**, **Cecil Sharp House**, **The Underworld**, **Dingwalls** and **The Camden Assembly**, there's a show or a club night for everyone here, most nights of the week.

EAT

This is not a gourmet neighbourhood, but try your luck at the Camden Market street-food stalls: **The Cheese Wheel** and **Yorkshire Burrito** are Insta-famous and **Pino's Warung** is great for Indonesian bites. **Sushi Salsa** does a good-value all-you-can-eat menu. Or keep the gothic vibes flowing with vampire-themed **Lost Souls Pizza**.

DRINK

The classic metalhead hangout is 'the Dev' (**The Devonshire Arms**), while Amy Winehouse was a regular at indie watering hole **The Hawley Arms. The Constitution** has a canalside beer garden that's worth knowing about and **Werewolf Beer** is always fun – as you'd expect from a taproom themed like a fairground ghost train.

SHOP

Ravewear purveyors **Cyberdog**, original Doc Martens stockists the **British Boot Company**, backstreet bookshop **Walden** and Portuguese deli **Ferreira** are all stalwarts. Record shops are also big here – try **All Ages** for punk, **Raven** for metal, **Massive International** for reggae, and **Out on the Floor** and **Rock 'n' Roll Rescue** for second-hand gems of all genres.

Above: British Boot Company; KOKO
Below: Camden Lock

Wednesday! deli
rket.com/DILI
ENTRANCE
WAY OUT
CHEESE STEAK
CANALSIDE BAR

Camden Lock

JONGLEURS
LOCK 17
17
THE NIGHT MARKET
EVERY THURSDAY 7TH AUG - 4TH SEPT UNTIL 10PM
CAMDENLOCKMARKET.COM
CAMDEN LOCK DINGWALL
Get involved
join us

17

CROUCH END

Family-focused, well-to-do north London enclave

Plenty of London neighbourhoods feel like villages, but that's truer of Crouch End than most. Residential and relaxed, its Victorian backstreets are home to a clutch of showbiz types, alongside countless well-heeled north London families. This is the kind of place where you're always bumping into your neighbours – usually on The Broadway, where all roads seem to lead. Its terraces of independent shops, restaurants and cafes owe at least some of their turnover to the fact that it's notoriously hard to leave, given the lack of Tubes and the hilly trek to even the nearest Overground stations. That goes for getting there too – but Crouch End's boutique-y vibe and unique businesses make it worth the schlep. And once you're done, head to nearby Queen's Wood, Alexandra Palace Park or the Parkland Walk. The latter is a green stroll along an overgrown ex-railway line that runs the 2.5 miles from Highgate to Finsbury Park.

●

DO

Catch a movie at the independent **ArtHouse** cinema or a stand-up set **Downstairs at the King's Head** (making Crouch Enders cackle since 1981). Jump into the open-air **Park Road Lido**. And keep an eye on modernist landmark **Hornsey Town Hall**, reopening in stages as an arts centre and hotel.

EAT

Brunch at **Beam**, **Rosemary** or **Brunch on the Hill**. Stop for a lunchtime sandwich at old-school, family-run **Dunns**, bagel specialists **North & Ten** or the legendary **Max's Sandwich Shop**. Book in for dinner at **Les Associes**, an eccentric French spot that feels like dining in someone's living room.

DRINK

The Queens is N8's essential local boozer, all wood panelling and stained glass. **Small Beer** serves the craft ale contingent admirably, while **Little Mercies** draws cocktail fans from all over London and **The Cellars** makes wine-drinkers very happy indeed.

SHOP

Pick up kids' books at **Pickled Pepper** (which also hosts a children's theatre), toys at **Niddle Noddle** (it has a slide!) and clothes at **Mini Kin**. Hunt for antiques at **Junk N8 Disorderly** and **Little Paris**. Sniff out the finest cheese at **Jumi** or candles and soaps at **Mahala** and **No 46 Park Road**. And scratch your vinyl itch at **Flashback Records**.

Above: Beam; Pickled Pepper
Below: Niddle Noddle; Park Road Lido

18

KING'S CROSS

Former industrial district turned shopping destination

Not long ago, King's Cross was a semi-abandoned wasteland of empty warehouses, canals and cobbled alleys. By day, commuters got in and out as quickly as they could; at night, it was the domain of sex workers and wide-eyed clubbers. But you'd hardly know that today, walking through what could be the most radically transformed neighbourhood in the whole city. Fashion students, shoppers, office workers and Harry Potter fans stroll up and down shiny boulevards, beep in and out of huge glass blocks, browse trendy boutiques, sit at pavement cafes and throng the concourses of King's Cross and St Pancras stations (both of which have had architectural glow-ups). Urban explorers and ex-ravers might mourn the loss of the old King's Cross, but it's hard not to get swept up in the excitement of the new 'KX' – and there's still no shortage of interesting stuff going on in the less-regenerated backstreets around King's Cross station.

•

DO

Explore the UK's LGBTQ+ history at **Queer Britain** museum; watch a movie at the **Everyman** (or outdoors by the canal in summer) or a sound-and-light show at **Lightroom**; catch an indie gig at **Scala** or a folk night at **Jamboree**; book a sightseeing boat trip from the **London Canal Museum**; then seek peace at the idyllic **Camley Street Natural Park**.

EAT

KX's new-build areas are packed with restaurants, from meze at **Bubala** and pizza at **Happy Face** to the posh Spanish grill **Parrillan**. But the older streets are also well worth a stroll at dinner time, especially if you're after Thai (**Supawan**), Malaysian (**Hawker's Kitchen**), Cantonese (**Dim Sum Duck** – be ready to queue) or vegan Japanese food at **Itadakizen**.

DRINK

Two of London's best pubs are tucked away around here: the tiny **King Charles I** and craft beer specialists **The Queen's Head**. For more continental vibes, check out **Vermuteria** at Coal Drops Yard, then head to audiophile bars **Supermax** or **Spiritland** till late.

SHOP

In an area full of post-industrial reinventions, **Coal Drops Yard** stands out: a former railway depot now home to a collection of upmarket brands and boutiques. Don't miss the shops along **Lower Stable Street** or **Word on the Water,** London's only bookshop on a boat.

Word on the Water

Coal Drops Yard

19

TOTTENHAM

Diverse, community-focused north London heartland

The vast sweep of Tottenham is as multicultural as they come. Proudly working class since day one, it's welcomed successive waves of immigration, its well-established Caribbean and African population joined by South Americans, Turks and Eastern Europeans. The community spirit is exemplified at Seven Sisters Indoor Market (a.k.a. the Latin Village), a city-wide gathering place for residents from across Latin America and beyond that recently triumphed in a decade-long battle against closure. Further up the High Road, the hulking Tottenham Hotspur Stadium hosts big gigs (Beyoncé is a regular) as well as big-league football. Despite the glint of the stadium, Tottenham still has a reputation for being rough around the edges. Who knows how long it'll last? N17 has been designated 'up-and-coming' for a few years now, and microbreweries and minimalist cafes have sprouted on its high streets and industrial estates. For now, it's still a refreshing alternative to its more gentrified neighbours.

Tottenham Hotspur Stadium and OOF Gallery

DO

The beautiful game? It is at **OOF Gallery**: the world's first contemporary art space dedicated to football. Elsewhere in Tottenham, you can rave in an old Ikea (**Drumsheds**) and a rum warehouse (**Distillery**) or fall on your bum to a funky beat at **Roller Nation**, London's only permanent roller disco.

EAT

Beyoncé-approved 'Nigerian tapas' joint **Chuku's** and more down-to-earth Ghanaian cafe **Gina's** proudly rep Tottenham's West African community. For Asian flavours, head to **Hochima** (Vietnamese) and **Makimayo** (Japanese), and for European small plates, **Pasero**.

DRINK

It's a beer-drinker's paradise. There's a plethora of good pubs, from the community-run **Antwerp Arms** to the buzzing **Beehive**, the country-style **Ferry Boat Inn** and the roast-slinging **High Cross**. And the brewery taproom scene is immaculate: **Redemption**, **Bohem** and **Gravity Well** cluster up north, while **Mother Kelly's** and **Pressure Drop** are found near Tottenham Hale Tube. Meanwhile, **Coulure** and **Perkyn's** are your go-tos for wine.

SHOP

Stock up on frozen dumplings at the massive **Loon Fung** supermarket and Caribbean ingredients at **Cinnamon Leaf Food Hall**. Then try on a new (old) jacket at **Vibe Vintage** and head to the lovely cafe/deli **With Milk** to pick up sourdough, pastries and some posh tins.

Above: OOF Gallery; Pressure Drop Taproom
Below: With Milk; Chuku's

20

HIGHBURY

Gourmet corner of residential Islington

Over the last ten years, this residential corner of north London has become one of the foodiest bits of the city. It might have started with the clutch of independents on Highbury Barn (butcher, cheesemonger, fishmonger, deli), or maybe the opening of pasta purveyors Trullo at Highbury Corner in 2010. But things have accelerated since 2015, with restaurant after acclaimed restaurant setting up shop in the area. (Further credentials: Jamie Oliver moved his company HQ here in 2017 and Nigel Slater is a long-time local.) 'Eating out' now rivals 'going to see the Arsenal' as a reason for Londoners to make the journey to Highbury. Besides the restaurants, there's plentiful parklife, pubs and cafes, independent shops and proximity to more fun and culture – especially where Highbury nudges up against its neighbours Canonbury and Finsbury Park. While you're here, look out for the topiary animals dotted around the area's front gardens: the charitable work of local hedge-trimming hero Tim Bushe.

●

Highbury Fields

DO

Catch a gig at **Union Chapel** or Friday-night comedy at **T-Bird Bar** or see the latest show at the **Estorick Collection of Modern Italian Art**, in a lovely Georgian villa.

EAT

Where to start? There's natural wine and small plates at **Top Cuvée** and **Westerns Laundry**, while **Sambal Shiok** serves fiery laksa in low-key digs. **Fink's** cafe is a local institution, **Xi'an Impression** is legendary for its hand-pulled noodles and **The Plimsoll** has turned an old Irish pub into a gastro destination. At the other end of the spectrum, **The Hope** has been serving fry-ups since 1937 and **Baban's Naan** dishes out tandoori flatbreads from a tiny, tiled shop. If you find yourself hungry in Highbury, you're not trying hard enough.

DRINK

Have a glass of vino at the cheery wine bar **The Nook**, drink a spritz in the sun at **Highbury Library** or stop for a cup of genmaicha outside **Kissa Wa Café**.

SHOP

Stock up your larder at **Highbury Barn**, particularly **La Fromagerie** and **Da Mario** deli – and stop for babka at **One Root Bakery**. Then shop for books: **Ink@84** sells stylish titles and stationery, while **House of Hodge** is a more chaotic second-hand selection – and nearby **BookBar** lets you pair your read with a glass of something.

Above: Union Chapel; Fink's
Below: BookBar; The Plimsoll

21

HAMPSTEAD

*Rarefied north London neighbourhood
with a famous heath*

Sitting on one of the capital's highest points, Hampstead is lofty in more ways than one. It has a reputation as London's Olympus: a neighbourhood of the great and good, from Sigmund Freud to George Michael. With dozens of blue plaques, red-brick townhouses and black-tiled street signs, Hampstead's distinguished air is instantly palpable from a walk along its winding, climbing streets. The people here are well-heeled (and strong-calved, thanks to all those steep hills). Posh chains and lots of places to buy matcha and fancy kitchenware cluster around the Tube station. Up on the 'mount' there are full-on mansions, while other backstreets are lined with honey-coloured Georgian cottages with tidy front gardens. A little further down the hill is the 'village', with yet another lovely high street. And that's before you even get to the epic expanse of Hampstead Heath, with its acres of grass and woods, bathing ponds and stately home.

●

Hampstead Heath

DO

Pay homage to Hampstead residents past by poking around their gaffs: the **Freud Museum**, **Keats House**, the **Isokon Gallery** and **2 Willow Road** (former home of Ernő Goldfinger). **Hampstead Pergola** was built for soap tycoon Lord Leverhulme, and there's more splendour on display, including Rembrandts and Vermeers, at **Kenwood House**. If all that grandeur makes you depressed about your flat, soothe yourself with a dip in one of the heath's three **bathing ponds** or some chin-stroking at **Camden Art Centre**.

EAT

For lunch without spending a fortune, choose between bagels from **Olive & Sage**, the delightfully old-school **Coffee Cup** or Japanese yakitori bar **Jin Kichi**. **L'Antica Pizzeria** is a strong option too, and there are always queues at **La Crêperie de Hampstead**.

DRINK

Another neighbourhood that's famous for its pubs, Hampstead boasts some stunners: the tucked-away **Holly Bush**, atmospheric **Spaniards Inn** (the perfect base for heath walks) and genteel **Garden Gate** are just three local classics.

SHOP

Fill your larder with fruit and veg at grocers **Artichoke**, bread and pastries at **Boulangerie Bon Matin**, and all sorts of deli goodies at **Bayley & Sage, The Hampstead Butcher & Providore** and **Giacobazzi's** down the hill.

Above: The Holly Bush; Hampstead Heath
Below: The Flask; Sayeh & Galton Flowers

Above: the Mixed Bathing Pond; Below: Kenwood House
Opposite: Hampstead Pergola

22

BOW & VICTORIA PARK VILLAGE

East End neighbours sharing a huge back garden

Sliced up by canals, railway lines and the roaring A12, Bow's jumble of terraces and council estates centres on Roman Road, where you can pick up a plate of pie and mash and a pair of net curtains as easily as a matcha latte and a Sally Rooney novel. It's quite a contrast to nearby Victoria Park Village – a slice of suburban Hackney complete with butcher, baker, grocer, toy shop and deli, plus an abundance of very decent post-park pubs. It's a lovely little neighbourhood, albeit quite a trek to the nearest station for the few locals who don't cycle everywhere. Between Bow and the Village lies Victoria Park itself, where east London's many communities come together for a stroll, an ice cream and a turn on the pedalos.

●

Victoria Park

<u>DO</u>

Victoria Park is always a crowd-pleaser, and not just for its summer music festivals. With its lakes, playgrounds, cafes, lawns, wooded walks, pagoda and Sunday food market, it's a proper East End gem. If it's raining, check out the latest show at **Chisenhale Gallery** instead.

<u>EAT</u>

Roman Road has an incredible cafe scene, from the trendy (like **Mae + Harvey**, peddlers of stacked sandwiches and brunch classics) to the traditional (the cash-only gem that is **Randolfi's**, where staff dish up slices of cake for less than a quid). For a proper meal, book in at airy pizzeria **Lanterna** or **Polentina**, an Italian lunch spot inside a sustainable clothing workshop.

<u>DRINK</u>

A chai by the lake in Victoria Park from **Pavilion Cafe** never goes amiss, but if it's booze you're after, head to **The Palm Tree**: a fantastic old-school (cash-only) boozer standing alone by the canal. If you're lucky, you'll catch the house swing band playing live. North of the park, you've got the massive beer garden at **People's Park Tavern** and the ever-buzzy **Hemingway**.

<u>SHOP</u>

The curation is impeccable at **Bàrd Books**, which also has a cosy cafe and runs plenty of events. Head to Fish Island for second-hand furniture galore from **Lofty's** or **Aelfred**. In Victoria Park Village, stock up your pantry at **The Deli Downstairs** and your bathroom cabinet at **big.**

Above: Polentina; The Deli Downstairs
Below: Aelfred; Bàrd Books

23

STRATFORD

Local hub transformed by the 2012 Olympics

Everything changed for Stratford on 6 July 2005: the day London won the 2012 Olympic Games. Cranes sprouted in the Lea Valley. Housing, allotments and green space were bulldozed, along with post-industrial curios like 'Fridge Mountain' (at 20 feet tall, supposedly the biggest collection of discarded white goods in Europe). In their place: a park full of swish sporting venues, a high-speed rail station, slick new flats and a titanic shopping centre. The construction keeps coming: the V&A has opened two offshoots and even Camden's Jazz Cafe has announced a forthcoming Stratford outpost. The merits of the Olympic legacy are still debated – especially its impact on the people who called Stratford home before the Games. But there's no doubt that 2012 turned Stratford into a destination and there's a *lot* to do around here these days.

●

DO

The **V&A East Storehouse** lets you check out stored objects close up, including David Bowie's personal archive; **Sadler's Wells East** hosts all sorts of dance shows; and you can whizz down the world's longest tunnel slide at the **ArcelorMittal Orbit**. Beyond the park, there's the venerable **Stratford East** theatre.

EAT

Brash Italian diner **Super Club Roma** serves up enough good vibes to (almost) make you forget you're in Westfield. Across the road in **Stratford Centre**, the **5 Continents** food court serves global dishes at more down-to-earth prices – or head upmarket with dinner at floating eatery **Barge East** or posh Japanese joint **Kokin**, with its panoramic terrace.

DRINK

Darkhorse and **Hand Cafe** are standouts on a decent cafe scene along Victory Parade and there's a branch of **e5 Bakehouse** at the V&A East Storehouse. Later, order a cocktail at queer-friendly cafe/bar **Tina We Salute You**, play a board game at **Escape Bar** or keep it old-school at the super-trad **King Edward VII** pub.

SHOP

Venture into **Westfield** if you dare. But if not, there's a delightful kids' bookshop at the **Discover Children's Story Centre**. Buy bits and bobs alongside the locals at **Stratford Market Village** or sustainable groceries at **Refill Therapy**.

V&A East Storehouse

Barge East

24

SHOREDITCH & SPITALFIELDS

No longer trendy, but still a vibe

It was the byword for noughties cool, but Shoreditch these days is no longer where you'll find London's art kids shaping the latest subcultures (in between big nights out). In fact, on Friday and Saturday nights, it can seem like nothing more than a neon-lit wilderness of stag parties. But with its post-gentrification legacy of stylish shops, restaurants and hotels, Shoreditch is still well worth a day's wander – especially in combination with Spitalfields, its neighbour on the fringes of the City of London. Here you'll find historic Georgian streets cheek by jowl with the curry houses, vintage stores and Sunday market stalls of Brick Lane.

CITY
SRICE
OPEN
TILL
LATE
ALADIN
Vintage
MARKET
LONDON'S
VINTAGE
MECCA
OPEN SEVEN
DAYS A WEEK
OPEN
ENTRANCE

Brick Lane

<u>DO</u>

Poke around the **Museum of the Home** to see how Londoners have lived over the centuries, visit the goats at **Spitalfields City Farm**, take a tour of **Dennis Severs' House**, an eccentric time warp in a Georgian townhouse, and see the Huguenot buildings on **Fournier Street**.

<u>EAT</u>

Pick between Brick Lane's two famous beigel (not bagel) shops or have brunch at antipodean joints **Ozone** or **Lantana**. **Smoking Goat** serves up reliably brilliant Thai drinking food and **Brat** is a gourmet mainstay. **The Kitchens at Old Spitalfields Market** offer a rotating selection of street food, from yakitori to kebabs.

<u>DRINK</u>

Grab a coffee from **Allpress** or **Nude** to fortify your wanderings or pop into **Bike Shed Moto Co** for a beer with the bikers. **Discount Suit Company** is a cute subterranean speakeasy, while **The Pride of Spitalfields** is an excellent backstreet boozer.

<u>SHOP</u>

Brick Lane and the former **Truman Brewery** explode each weekend with stalls and pop-ups, while the Thursday antiques selection at **Spitalfields Market** is particularly good. **World of Echo** and **Flashback** are crate-digging hotspots. Swing by **The Common Press** for nicely curated books (plus a calendar of welcoming LGBTQ+ community events) before browsing the fashion and homeware boutiques along **Redchurch Street**.

Above: Dennis Severs' House; The Kitchens at Old Spitalfields Market
Below: Brick Lane Beigel Shop; The Common Press

ELEVEN

ELEVEN AND A HALF
Fournier Street

25

LONDON FIELDS

Street food and parklife: an east London enclave

Once upon a time, London Fields was little more than a local park surrounded by quiet Victorian streets, halfway between Dalston and Hackney Central. Now it's a bona fide destination, where, every weekend, locals walking their dogs and toddlers mix with party kids walking off last night's excesses and fashionista couples clutching coffee and pastries. Why are people drawn here from across east London and beyond? The answers are many: the cafes, shops and stalls of Broadway Market and Netil Market; the foodie hotspots that have popped up along the canal and under the railway; the great pubs; and, crucially, the park itself, with its ample lawns, wildflower meadow and heated, Olympic-sized outdoor pool. Join the crowd, why don't you?

●

FISH
CHIPS
Please
gum

DO

Take a dip in **London Fields Lido**, of course, and dry out in the park – or at **Netil House's Rooftop Sauna. The Viktor Wynd Museum of Curiosities** includes taxidermy, outsider art, global artefacts and bodily bits from celebrities dead and alive.

EAT

You're spoiled for choice. Basque-style oven-roasted turbot at **Brat x Climpson's Arch**? Home-cooked lunches at **e5 Bakehouse**? Gourmet deli delights at **Oren**? Queue-worthy falafel from **Pockets**? Kid-friendly udon noodles at **Koya Ko**? Or – at the weekend – the stalls of **Broadway Market**? You could eat every meal out for a week and still have plenty to try.

DRINK

The pub scene here is at its best in summer: a midweek alfresco pint outside the backstreet **Prince Arthur** is a thing of beauty and **Wilton Way Deli** serves sundowners on one of the area's most picturesque thoroughfares. The bars aren't bad either: try **Diddy's** for cocktails and fun tunes, **Helgi's** or **Saint Monday** for beer and heavy metal, **Yuki** or **Binch** for wine and **Netil360** for views.

SHOP

Fill your trendy tote with house-smoked salmon from **Secret Smokehouse**, books from **Donlon**, **Artwords** and **The Broadway Bookshop**, cardamom buns from **Pavilion** and art supplies from **Atlantis**, plus whatever takes your fancy along **Broadway Market**'s many varied stalls.

Above: London Fields Lido
Below: Koya Ko; Donlon Books

Above: Artwords
Opposite: Broadway Market

26

DALSTON

The hip, multicultural heart of Hackney

To understand Dalston, take a walk down its central thoroughfare: Kingsland Road and Kingsland High Street. In the late noughties, this was London's undisputed hipster heartland, dotted with clubs and dubbed 'The Strip'. Only a few survivors cling on, notably 24-hour queer spot Dalston Superstore. But when the party kids are sleeping it off, Dalston's main drag serves communities that have been here longer, with buzzing Turkish restaurants and Afro-Caribbean shops. Ridley Road Market has everything you need, from halal butchers to watch repairs, hot Caribbean food to hip cocktails. There's more to explore in Gillett Square, a gathering spot where trendy ventures (like Brunswick East cafe and the NTS digital radio station) sit alongside local stalwarts like Kaffa Coffee. Residential streets stretch either side – a jumble of poshed-up Victorian terraces and council estates that typifies the contradictions of Dalston, and indeed the whole of London.

●

Ridley Road Market

EAST

DO

Try indie theatre at the **Arcola**, live jazz at **Vortex** and **Dalston Jazz Bar,** films at the **Rio Cinema**, big gigs at **EartH**, small ones at **The Shacklewell Arms**, experimental music at **Cafe OTO** and drag nights at **Dalston Superstore**. Looking for green space? **Dalston Eastern Curve Garden** is a blissful oasis.

EAT

There's no end of Turkish food in Dalston, but two good options are **Mangal 1**, for classics in a no-frills setting, or its upmarket little sibling, **Mangal 2**. Elsewhere, **Andu Cafe** serves a delicious Ethiopian platter for around a tenner a head and **Little Duck The Picklery** is a small-plates joint with a focus on fermentation. The sandwiches at **The Dusty Knuckle** are legendary.

DRINK

Take a cocktail crawl down London's 'mezcal mile', a string of margarita bars that extends north from **Hacha** via **Corrochio's, Tipsy, Del74** and **Viva** (plus **Doña** in Stoke Newington, no.15). For traditionalists, **The Army & Navy** is an unassuming old-school backstreet pub that has been named London's best boozer, and **40FT Brewery** reps the local craft beer scene.

SHOP

Grab groceries from **Ridley Road Market** and cash-and-carry institution **TFC**; hit up **Beyond Retro, L.F.Markey** and **Positive Retail** for garms old and new; and shop for vinyl at **Eldica, Recycle Vinyl** and **Hidden Sounds**.

Above: L.F.Markey
Below: Andu Cafe; The Dusty Knuckle

Above: Rio Cinema
Opposite: Little Duck The Picklery

27

BETHNAL GREEN

The epitome of the East End

A bastion of the classic East End, Bethnal Green was the territory of the villainous Kray twins back in the '60s. Although pockets of it are now very posh, including the super-picturesque Jesus Hospital Estate area around Columbia Road, the wider area is still much grittier (and a notch more affordable) than its near-neighbours, Shoreditch (no.24) and Hackney. The big Bangladeshi population is obvious from a stroll along the stalls of Bethnal Green Road – one of the two major east–west routes. The other is Hackney Road, where fancy wine bars, cafes and restaurants sit side by side with wholesale shops selling suitcases and cleaning supplies. It's the kind of contrast that's everywhere in this many-faced neighbourhood: Victorian terraces and Brutalist landmarks, quiet parks and traffic-choked high streets, trendy boutiques and cockney pubs that seem to have hardly changed since the Krays' day.

Campania & Jones

DO

Check out the nostalgic displays of toys and other kids' artefacts at **Young V&A**, where on a rainy day you'll spot half of east London's parent population. (If that's you, nearby **Hackney City Farm** is also well worth a shout.) Hit up a queer cabaret party at **Bethnal Green Working Men's Club**, see politicised art and photography at **Four Corners** or **Auto Italia** and go for a bargain spa day at local institution **York Hall**.

EAT

Round here you can get anything from a quintessential East End fry-up – in the art-deco splendour and chatty atmosphere of British-Italian caff **E. Pellicci**, a family business since 1900 – to the double-Michelin-starred tasting menu at **Da Terra**. Hit up **Campania & Jones** for pasta, **Brawn** for modern British cooking, **Ozone** for Aussie brunch and lamingtons, the **Marksman** for a best-in-class roast, **The Gallery Cafe** for homely vegetarian goodness, **Flat Earth** for weird-but-they-work pizzas (try the kimchi fiorentina!), **Bistrotheque** for all-day dining in a fabulously welcoming warehouse conversion or **A Portuguese Love Affair** for Lusitanian classics – including a barnstorming pastel de nata.

DRINK

This is old-school pub territory, and **The Camel, Florist Arms, Approach Tavern, King's Arms** and **Royal Oak** all keep it pleasingly classic – but there's also the all-embracing kitsch of **The Queen Adelaide**, the smart **Sun Tavern** or the hard-partying **Star of Bethnal Green**,

Above: Flat Earth Pizzas; Hackney City Farm
Below: Jesus Hospital Estate houses; Bethnal Green Working Men's Club

if you want to shake things up. For cocktails, hit up
Satan's Whiskers; for Parisian chic, try **Printers &**
Stationers.

SHOP

Columbia Road on a Sunday is a major London draw: the
flower traders set up at crack of sparrows to flog truck-
loads of blooms and houseplants to the coffee-clutching
throngs, with prices dipping in the late afternoon. Along
here you'll also find hip deli **Hackney Essentials**, nifty
craft shops like **Milagros** and **Straw**, and nearby **Yo-Yo**
Records and **Crypt of the Wizard**, catering to very different constituencies of vinyl fans. Other great shops in
the wider neighbourhood include tucked-away bakery
BreidBakers, artist-run Italian deli **4Cose** and **Plant**
Warehouse – for getting your botanical fix if it isn't
market day on Columbia Road.

Columbia Road Flower Market

28

LEYTON &
LEYTONSTONE

Hip, residential and still (just)
flying under the radar

More low-key and low-rise than neighbouring Walthamstow (no.30), this part of London is a wash of terraces
from the Lea Valley to the southern tip of Epping Forest,
bisected by the concrete trench of the A12. Along with
old-school East Enders and long-established Romanian
and South Asian communities, E10 and E11 are increas-
ingly home to young, trendy families – and businesses.
Stroll down the pedestrianised stretch of Francis Road
or along the railway arches next to Midland Road station, and you could easily think you're in London Fields
(no.25) or Peckham (no.37). But what makes Leyton and
Leytonstone distinct is the relaxed, slightly suburban
community vibe: everyone knows local characters like
Percy the Francis Road cat, and institutions like drag
Sundays at the Northcote Arms and local newsletter
Leytonstoner have been going strong for yonks.

Phlox BOOKS
BOOKS • BOOZE • COFFEE
BOOKS
BOOZE
COFFEE
10 - 6pm

DO

Get your skates on at the **Lea Valley Ice Centre**, cheer on local heroes **Leyton Orient FC**, get green-fingered at **Leyton Boundary Community Garden**, try pottery at **Turning Earth** or row a boat across **Hollow Ponds**.

EAT

Tuck into home-style vegan food at the **Hornbeam Community Cafe** or the legendary haggis toastie at **Deeney's**. **Loop** hosts impressive chefs for all-too-brief residencies. For pizza, try **Oscar's** or **Papi's Munchies**. The offbeat ice-cream flavours at **Chunk Provisions** draw queues (try the peanut butter and jelly) and the bakery scene thrives: tick off **Wins**, **Tun** and **Wild Goose** on your tasty tour.

DRINK

There's a heady array of taprooms around here, with **Blondies Brewery**, **Gravity Well** and **Libertalia**, plus a cluster on the Argall Avenue industrial estate. **The Heathcote & Star** and the **North Star** make for a mini-constellation of community-focused pubs – and of course, there's a decent natty wine spot, **Swirl E10**. For coffee, try **Back to Ours** after a walk on Wanstead Flats.

SHOP

Vinyl paradise **Dreamhouse Records**, deli-cafe **Yardarm**, **Phlox Books** and long-serving florist **George's Den** make Francis Road a go-to. Nearby, **Quinto** sells an intriguing edit of second-hand books and there's often a must-shop pop-up at **Host**.

Yardarm

29

LOWER CLAPTON

*Fashionable families, indie shopping
and wild marshland*

Head eastwards from Dalston or Hackney Central to Clapton and you'll be following in the footsteps of countless young families and renters in their quest for more space and a slightly more suburban vibe. That's given Lower Clapton (south of Lea Bridge Road) a reputation as a land of natty wine, Lime bikes and Birkenstock clogs. It's not entirely unjustified: you'll spot as many fashion kids and Bugaboo-pushing creative-industry parents around here as anywhere in London, popping in and out of the wine bars, indie boutiques, hyped restaurants and posh grocers. But like almost anywhere in Hackney, there's huge diversity in Lower Clapton – most visibly around Chatsworth Road, where pavement cafes sit alongside pound shops and Caribbean takeaways, and terraced streets of done-up Victorian houses meet the mid-century council estates that sprawl down the hill to the Lee Navigation canal and Hackney Marshes.

●

Chatsworth
Road E5

DO

There's no end of fun in Clapton. Catch a screening at the excellent **Castle Cinema** or in the tiny back room at **Umit & Son**, an Aladdin's cave of analogue film. See a gig at raucous dive bar **Blondies**, speakeasy pub **Biddle Bros**, former library **Chats Palace** or one of three musical churches: **St John at Hackney**, the **Round Chapel** and **St James the Great** (also known as the Church of Sound). Poke around the well-preserved Tudor manor, **Sutton House**. Take a pottery class at **SkandiHus**. Or embrace green space with a big old stomp around **Hackney Marshes**.

EAT

Lower Clapton Road is a gourmet thoroughfare, with Asian food especially well represented: Chinese with a twist at **Lucky & Joy**, elevated Malaysian at **Mambow**, laid-back Vietnamese at **Hai Café** and dim sum at **My Neighbours the Dumplings** – plus superb sushi at nearby **Uchi**. Over on Chatsworth Road, there's more good stuff: Jamaican stalwart **People's Choice**, cosy lunches at **Dorée & Co**, quality pasta at **Leo's** and abundant street food at the excellent Sunday market.

DRINK

You can sip on new-wave wine at **107** or cocktails at **Dovetail** – but Lower Clapton is best for proper pubs. Whether it's at community boozers **The Elderfield** or **The Clapton Hart**, buzzy canalside spot **The Princess of Wales** or party pub **The Star By Hackney Downs**, there's a bar here for everyone to prop up.

Pages of Hackney

Eat 17 is a wonderland of gourmet groceries, while **Clapton Craft** stocks beer from hundreds of indie breweries. Further up Chatsworth Road you'll find all sorts of trinkets and gifts for kids at **Triangle** and for dogs at **Pack and Clowder** or **Hackney Barkers**. Vinyl-heads can lose hours at **Jelly Records** and **Atlantis Records**, while homeware-hunters should hit up **Rooms, Urban Primitives** and **Mad Atelier** – plus **Conservatory Archives** for the houseplants of your dreams. And let's not forget bookseller **Pages of Hackney** and yarn shop **Wild and Woolly**: friendly hubs for (possibly overlapping) communities of readers and knitters.

Above: Uchi
Opposite: The Clapton Hart

30

WALTHAMSTOW

*Sprawling outer London neighbourhood
full of local pride*

Less a single neighbourhood, more a veritable town, Walthamstow is almost an island. It's hemmed in by barriers both natural (the marshy valley of the River Lea; the southernmost strip of Epping Forest) and man-made (the roaring North Circular). No wonder it has such a strong local identity, celebrated in dozens of colourful murals by the Wood Street Walls project. In fact, there are (at least) three Walthamstows. There's the multicultural, working-class suburb most visible along Hoe Street and Walthamstow Market. There's the new Walthamstow: trendy in a genteel way, populated by space-seeking arrivals from Hackney. That's the vibe in Walthamstow Village, with its quiet high street, leafy main square, cottages and almshouses. And then there's the warehouse district: an area carpeted with post-industrial space to make stuff happen, whether it's a microbrewery, a metal-working studio or a purveyor of local honey.

●

Gods Own Junkyard

<u>DO</u>

The creations of local hero Chris Bracey, an incredible designer of neon signs, draw justified crowds to the **Gods Own Junkyard** warehouse. You can celebrate another local legend, the designer William Morris, at his family home (now the **William Morris Gallery**) and garden (now the excellent **Lloyd Park**). Catch a show at **Soho Theatre Walthamstow**, which revamped the old Granada cinema in 2025 to present a packed programme of big comedy names, or drop in on the wild variety of fun – from soul discos to queer cabaret – hosted at **Walthamstow Trades Hall**. Learn about local history at the dinky **Vestry House Museum** or industrial heritage at the **Walthamstow Pumphouse Museum**. Then go for a big old mooch in the splendid **Walthamstow Wetlands** nature reserve.

<u>EAT</u>

If it's Hackney-style trendy small plates you want, **Slow-Burn** is the place to head. But elsewhere there's a feast of relaxed options, from the local outposts of **Sodo** and **Yard Sale** for pizza, to **Etles** for Central Asian Uyghur cooking, to brunch spot **Bühler + Co**, gastropub **The Castle** and the very popular **Lloyd Park** street-food market each Saturday (plus the stalls with seating at shipping-container market **CRATE St James Street**). **The Coven of Wiches** and **Mini Hiba** are worth the small schlep over to Wood Street. And you must stop by **Market Cafe** on the High Street: a greasy spoon that doubles as a shrine to Princess Diana.

Above: Walthamstow Wetlands; Walthamstow Village
Below: Soho Theatre Walthamstow; William Morris Gallery

DRINK

You like craft beer, right? Walthamstow serves gallons of the stuff and plenty of it is brewed right here. The litany of E17 taprooms includes **The Real Al Company, Pillars Brewery, Signature Brew, Pretty Decent Beer Co** and **Exale**, plus the mammoth **Big Penny Social**. Many of these are stops on the well-worn 'Blackhorse Beer Mile', where drinkers spill out onto the street alongside MOT garages and builders' merchants. There's even an urban winery here, **Renegade**, though make sure not to mix your drinks. Pub-wise, 'stow-dwellers are well served by **The Nags Head, Ye Olde Rose & Crown** and **The Chequers**. And grab a coffee from **HAVEN** or any of the mini-branches of local roasters **Perky Blenders**.

SHOP

Wander down the high street to browse Europe's longest open-air market, which sells everything from school shirts to saris. There's also a cluster of famous fabric shops and the eclectic **Stow Bazaar** indoor market, and nearby is one of two local branches of friendly indie grocers **Nourished Communities**. Head to the Village for something completely different: curated gifts, stationery and clothing from **The Little Mandarin, PAVEMENT, The W Store** and **Here On Earth**, plus cute kids' stuff at **WORD**. Wood Street's retro indoor market is worth a browse (pick up a pastry from **Wood Street Bakery**). Plus, for now at least, this area of London is still home to eccentric specialists like army surplus store **Eastman Camp**, vintage movie poster boutique **Reelstore** and **Krypton Komics**.

Wood Street Bakery

31

BATTERSEA

Surprisingly diverse riverside community

Battersea lies just across the river from ultra-swanky Chelsea. But don't be fooled by the Victorian splendour of Battersea Park, the cutesy riverside streets around Battersea Square, the 'nappy valley' of Northcote Road or the presence of London's only licensed heliport. Carved up by railway lines and punctuated by tower blocks and industrial zones, this place has done its time as a working-class inner-city neighbourhood, and has the radical heritage to show for it. It was home to Britain's first council estate, London's first Black mayor, and one of the UK's few Communist MPs. More recently, it gave rise to a clutch of leading pirate radio stations and the pioneering rap collective So Solid Crew. The estates that Asher D and Lisa Maffia called home are now being regenerated – and big changes have also come to the iconic Battersea Power Station. The brick monolith, which once supplied a fifth of London's power, has reopened as a luxe shopping centre surrounded by expensive flats.

Battersea Power Station

DO

Catch a show at **Battersea Arts Centre** in the old town hall, see a play at **Theatre503** above the Latchmere pub or party at **The Clapham Grand** (which, yes, is technically in Battersea). Take a turn around **Battersea Park**, stopping off at the Children's Zoo to see the meerkats and lemurs. Or, on a rainy day, take shelter in **Battersea Power Station**, where there's a cinema, ping-pong bar and indoor crazy golf, as well as all the shops.

EAT

Old-school Italian classics at **Captain Corelli**, gourmet pizza from **Flour to the People!**, modern French small plates at **Ploussard**, seafood by the river at **Wright Bros.** and all sorts of good eats at the power station's **Arcade Food Hall & Bar**.

DRINK

The Magic Garden is an eclectic indoor-outdoor kind of spot, while **The Thieves** brings the fun with karaoke, comedy and cabaret. **Paya and Horse** is Battersea's quirky, cosy Serbian-run local and **Battersea Brewery** runs a tucked-away taproom near the power station.

SHOP

Skip the chains at the power station and head to **Battersea Flower Station** instead: a lovely little garden centre that feels like a secret garden alongside the railway viaduct. A booming local pastry scene is anchored by **Mahali** and **August** bakeries.

Battersea Park

32

VAUXHALL

Underrated stop-off for food and fun

Just across the river from the splendour of Westminster, Vauxhall made its name in the 18th century, when its Pleasure Gardens drew in Regency aristocrats for evenings of music, fireworks displays and cavorting in the bushes. Nowadays, this neighbourhood just outside central London is a bit of a crossroads with a somewhat confusing reputation. It's famous for transport (it's bisected by railway lines and a roaring one-way system), espionage (the heavily fortified HQ of MI6 is, ironically, hard to miss), gay clubs and cricket – The Oval is just down the road. Even if you're not into any of those, you'd still be silly to pass through this underrated corner of south London without stopping to explore.

DO

By day: feed the sheep and goats at **Vauxhall City Farm**, play petanque in the **Pleasure Gardens**, relax in the **Harleyford Road Community Garden** or catch an exhibition at **Gasworks**. By night: party hard at **Royal Vauxhall Tavern**, **Eagle** or **Fire** – the three biggest stops on Vauxhall's LGBTQ+ nightlife scene.

EAT

The Boxer family is responsible for two of the big culinary draws here. Dad Charlie runs **Italo** deli, perfect on a sunny morning when it serves delicious sandwiches to alfresco tables on a beautiful, community-run garden square. Charlie's son Jackson is the chef at **Brunswick House**, an upmarket British restaurant in the eclectic surroundings of architectural salvage company LASSCO.

DRINK

A cup of Earl Grey at **Tea House Theatre** or a pint at **Mother Kelly's** craft beer archway or **The Black Dog** – a refined corner pub improbably namechecked in a Taylor Swift song. Or perhaps drinks with a Big Ben view at the **Tamesis Dock** boat-bar.

SHOP

All things Portuguese at **Madeira**. As well as an impeccably stocked deli – a whole arch lined with everything from olives to salt cod to madeira wine and obscure liqueurs – there's a bakery with some of London's best pasteis de nata, and a cafe and restaurant if you can't wait till you get home to fill your face.

Brunswick House

33

DULWICH & HERNE HILL

Leafy south London suburbia

Dulwich practically defines 'leafy', with acres of parkland, private-school playing fields, a golf course and even a riding school – plus a nesting colony of four-by-fours, often found blocking pavements in Dulwich Village. Sometimes it's hard to believe you're in Zone 3, not rural Oxfordshire. Next door, Herne Hill has its own green lung: Brockwell Park, with a lido, walled garden and miniature railway. But it's not just posh parklife around here. There's a respectable selection of restaurants, cafes, indie shops and culture spots – including the venerable Dulwich Picture Gallery, which dates way back to 1817 but keeps things fresh with a new artist-designed pavilion each summer. That's the kind of thing that makes Dulwich surprisingly *un*-dull – and an appealingly green alternative to its edgier northern neighbours.

Bell House Cottage, Dulwich Village

DO

Check out the latest exhibition at **Dulwich Picture Gallery** or tour the eccentrically beautiful **House of Dreams Museum**. (It's also not far to the excellent **Horniman Museum** of anthropology and natural history.) Take a dip in the refreshing chill of **Brockwell Lido**, catch a film at **East Dulwich Picturehouse** or get green-fingered at the **Centre for Wildlife Gardening**. And of course, cheer on local lower-league heroes Dulwich Hamlet FC at their **Champion Hill** ground.

EAT

Lordship Lane has more than its fair share of strong dining options, including gastropubs **The Palmerston** and **The Lordship**, brunchy spot **Spinach**, Georgian joint **Kartuli** and Japanese eatery **Yama Momo**. Nearby, **Norbert's** draws crowds for its rotisserie chicken and chips.

DRINK

Herne Hill cafe and shop **Lulu's** turns into a classy wine bar after dark, and it's not far from two very decent pubs: **The Half Moon** and **The Prince Regent**.

SHOP

Stock up on baked goods at **Bunhead** and **Dough Artisan Bakehouse**, both at Herne Hill, or **Eric's** in Dulwich. Pick up your next read at **Village Books**. And hit up the markets at **Herne Hill** and **North Cross Road** for crafty bits and pieces or **What Mother Made** for super-cute kids' stuff.

Above: Dulwich Picture Gallery; Lulu's
Below: What Mother Made; Horniman Museum

Horniman Museum Gardens

34

GREENWICH

Nautical and nice: a Royal Borough by the water

Ahoy, shipmates! Greenwich is a throwback to when Britannia ruled the waves. A royal residence since the Middle Ages, commanding the shipyards at Deptford (no.39) and Woolwich, it later became home to the splendid Old Royal Naval College, which trained British naval officers for more than a century. You can visit today, and nearby are the National Maritime Museum, the dry-docked sailing ship *Cutty Sark* and the Royal Observatory, where you can hop from one hemisphere to the other over the prime meridian. Tourists aplenty chart a course around this most nautical of neighbourhoods, but most visitors miss out on Greenwich's winding Georgian backstreets, the wild depths of Greenwich Park and the local spots around Maze Hill. The town centre is cute and the maritime stuff can be pretty awe-inspiring. But walk the Thames Path all the way to the Greenwich Peninsula, watching the cityscape shift slowly from baroque to sci-fi, and you'll see a very different side of this Royal Borough.

The Old Royal Naval College

Greenwich Park and the Old Royal Naval College

DO

See the sights: the breathtaking **Painted Hall** (a.k.a. Britain's Sistine Chapel) at the **Old Royal Naval College**, the paintings and grand staircase at the (free-to-visit) **Queen's House** and Nelson's bloodstained coat at the **National Maritime Museum**. Hike to the peninsula to admire the river views and see some very different art on the epic sculpture trail **The Line**, which starts here.

EAT

Goddards has been serving pie and mash since the Victorian era, and there are more British classics to be had at meaty specialist **Heap's Sausage Deli**. **Paul Rhodes Bakery** is great for takeaway treats to eat by the river, while the cinnamon bun from **Fingal's Bakery** is worth the walk over to Maze Hill. For a cheap-and-cheerful dinner, check out indie Vietnamese joint **Pho Street** or Nepalese neighbourhood restaurant **Mountain View**.

DRINK

It's all about riverside pints here, and the **Trafalgar Tavern** has it nailed, with nautical bunting hanging over the Thameside tables. **The Yacht** next door is more low-key, but cosier on grey days. Or try backstreet boozer **The Morden Arms** to escape the tourists.

SHOP

Beyond the dinky stalls of **Greenwich Market**, head to **Casbah Records** and the **Music & Video Exchange** for vinyl, **Greenwich Vintage Market** for garms and antiques and **Made in Greenwich** for locally made ceramics.

The Painted Hall at the Old Royal Naval College

35

BRIXTON

The spiritual home of Black British culture

When the *Empire Windrush* liner brought Caribbean immigrants to London in 1948, many of them settled in Brixton, and a generation of Black Brits grew up in the area's bomb-damaged terraces and newly built social housing. Nowadays, that working-class, multicultural history is preserved in the Black Cultural Archives on Windrush Square, opposite the iconic marquee of the Ritzy Cinema. But it also lives on in the buzz and rush of Brixton's street life, from the market stalls on Electric Avenue to the shops and cafes of Brixton Market, from the hubbub outside the Tube station to the many local protests over the years against police violence, squat evictions and gentrification. The birthplace of David Bowie, and namechecked in famous songs by The Clash and Eddy Grant, Brixton is also a magnet for music-lovers: live venues like the Academy and the Electric and clubs like Phonox draw big names and thousands of fans every week.

Brixton Village Market

DO

Catch the next big thing at the **Windmill Brixton** – a hub for south London music acts on the up – or check out **Ashby's Mill**, an *actual* windmill dating from Brixton's rural past.

EAT

You'll always eat well in Brixton. Caribbean flavours are plentiful, of course: **Maureen's Brixton Kitchen** and **Fish, Wings & Tings** are local favourites. You could also go Asian: **Kaosarn** is perfect for a no-frills BYOB Thai dinner and **Three Uncles** specialises in Cantonese roasted meats. Or peruse the abundant food options at **Pop Brixton** or **Brixton Village**.

DRINK

Sample local brews at **Brixton Brewery**'s taproom, sip a glass of orange in the **Naughty Piglets** basement bar or find the perfect spot in the enormous beer garden at **The Duke of Edinburgh**.

SHOP

Browse for bargains at **Bookmongers**, a treasure trove specialising in remaindered titles, or shop for inclusive books at **Round Table**. Buy goods from **The Black Farmer Farmshop** or houseplants and records at **HAUS**. Caribbean sounds can be found at **Supertone Records** and **Lion Vibes**.

Above: Ashby's Mill, also known as Brixton Windmill; Fish, Wings & Tings
Below: Three Uncles; Bookmongers

36

BERMONDSEY

Working-class neighbourhood full of insider spots

Bermondsey is big. This vast district stretches all the way east from London Bridge (no.40) to Rotherhithe and south from the Thames to Peckham (no.37). A lot of this acreage is taken up with estates and industrial spaces – plus The Den, home to London's most cheerfully despised football club: Millwall. But there are plenty of Bermondsey pockets worth exploring. Smart warehouse conversions cluster around Bermondsey Street and Shad Thames, hosting upmarket restaurants and art spaces. There's a multicultural cockney community along Tower Bridge Road and Southwark Park Road. Food producers and purveyors amass at Spa Terminus and Maltby Street. More than a dozen taprooms draw crowds to the Bermondsey Beer Mile. And nondescript warehouses in the South Bermondsey industrial estates host some of the city's finest nightlife. It's an eclectic mix which guarantees there's far more to Bermondsey than meets the eye.

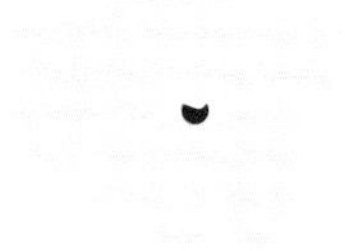

Bermondsey Antique Market

DO

Wander down Bermondsey Street to see what's on at the bright-pink **Fashion and Textile Museum** and the sleek **White Cube** gallery. Catch a play at the upmarket **Bridge Theatre** or kid-focused **Unicorn Theatre** and nose around **Gibbon's Rent** secret garden. After dark, head south-east to **Ormside Projects, Avalon Cafe** and **Venue MOT**: a triangle of venues that host some of the most exciting underground and electronic sounds in the city.

EAT

Bermondsey Street is a restaurant-hopper's world tour: from French at **Casse-Croûte** to Italian at **Cafe Murano**; Spanish at **José** to Japanese at **Hakata** and Malaysian at **Sentosa**. Meanwhile, **40 Maltby Street** is the standout spot in its foodie-focused row of railway arches.

DRINK

Boozing in Bermondsey? Hit the Beer Mile. **Anspach & Hobday, Cloudwater** and **The Kernel** are among the beer-nerd favourites here and there's even London's only sake taproom – **KANPAI** – with rice wine on tap.

SHOP

Bermondsey Antique Market, which starts eye-wateringly early every Friday, is one of the oldest in the city. There's also **Spa Terminus**, where you can pick up cheese, honey, ice cream, bread and loads more, straight from the wholesalers, every Friday and Saturday.

Above: Bermondsey Beer Mile; Spa Terminus
Below: 40 Maltby Street; Maltby Street Market

37

PECKHAM

The fast-changing heart of south London

Once upon a time, many knew Peckham as the home of iconic chancer Del Boy Trotter, from *Only Fools and Horses*. For others, it had a dark reputation as a hotbed of youth violence. Uniting these different visions was Peckham's status as a cast-iron working-class neighbourhood – though if you're really looking for a sitcom to represent SE15, try *Desmond's*, set in a Black barbershop. Peckham is the centre of African and Caribbean life in south London, with an especially strong Nigerian presence. But you'll spot something else too: a definite sense of the area changing. Since the late noughties, the familiar procession of artists, creative DINKYs ('dual income, no kids yet') and property speculators have gradually 'discovered' Peckham. Inevitably, it has become trendy. And as usual, that brings both the good (independent businesses doing cool, creative stuff) and the bad (rising rents). If Del Boy had held onto his council flat for a few more decades, he might have ended up a millionaire after all.

●

Bold Tendencies

<u>DO</u>

Explore London's hippest multistorey car park. At ground level: legendary cheap-as-chips cinema **Peckhamplex**. Above that: the workspaces and event venues of **Peckham Levels**. Cutting-edge gallery **Bold Tendencies** is next, followed by Peckham's crowning glory: massive rooftop bar **Frank's Cafe**. Virtually next door, **Copeland Park** and the **Bussey Building** are home to even more galleries, bars, studios, shops and big nights out. And for the morning-after stroll, explore the green expanses of **Peckham Rye Park** or **Burgess Park**.

<u>EAT</u>

Peckham does food very well across the whole price spectrum. Walk down Bellenden Road (the area's more villagey high street) for Thai at **The Begging Bowl**, Indian at **Ganapati** or Italian at **Artusi**. Stroll along Rye Lane for tacos at **Guacamoles** and **Taquiza**, Kurdish falafel at **Yada's** or adventurous Vietnamese at **Lai Rai**. Join the queue at legendary street-food spot **Suuyar** for a taste of proper Nigerian barbecue – or head to **805** restaurant, where local hero John Boyega famously brought his *Star Wars* co-star Harrison Ford to sample jollof rice, pounded yam and egusi.

<u>DRINK</u>

If you're drinking natural wine, **Forza Wine** and **Bar Levan** will keep you topped up. Prefer the pub? The classic option is **The Montpelier** but there's also **The Greyhound** (for big screens and DJ nights), the **Prince of Peckham** (for Caribbean food and party vibes) and

Above: Bold Tendencies; Ganapati
Below: Forza Wine; Peckhamplex

The view from Bold Tendencies' rooftop

low-key trendy hangout **The Peckham Pelican**. Fancy a cocktail? It's off to the listening bar **Jumbi** or the **Bussey Rooftop Bar**. Just want a coffee? Try minimalist **NOLA**, vegan **RONS** or social enterprise **Old Spike**.

SHOP

Wander the Aladdin's cave that is **Khan's Bargains** – you need it? They've got it! – then duck down **Holdrons Arcade** to check out the tiny independent shops and pop into **Etc.Store** for colourful homewares. Afro-Caribbean businesses predominate along busy Rye Lane, from cash-and-carries to takeaways and beauty parlours. Stock up on Persian ingredients at eclectic deli and restaurant **Persepolis**, then head down Bellenden Road for posh groceries at **General Store**. Finally, stop at **BOOKS** for its impeccable selection of... you can probably guess.

PERSEPOLIS
...FOR A TASTE OF PERSIA
FINE FOODS & HANDICRAFTS
30
PECKHAM
HIGH STREET
TEL
020·7639 8007
YOU SMILE
I SMILE
THEY SMILE
WE ALL SM
SMILE MORE PL
IRAN
PERSEPOLIS
OPEN

Persepolis

38

WATERLOO &
THE SOUTH BANK

Cultural monoliths and hidden gems

In 1951, the Festival of Britain transformed the bomb-shattered south side of the Thames into a monument to the UK's post-war recovery. Over the next 25 years, cultural venues sprang up along a new riverside pedestrian promenade. The modernist Royal Festival Hall, Queen Elizabeth Hall, Hayward Gallery and National Theatre were bold statements celebrating a forward-looking city – or concrete eyesores, depending on who you ask. Either way, they've become icons – and they've since been joined by the London Eye, the BFI IMAX and a whole host of other attractions, making this area one of the most well-trodden parts of the city. And it's not just the obvious landmarks that draw crowds: the Undercroft Skate Space is the grassroots home of British skateboarding, saved from destruction by a community campaign, and the Leake Street tunnel is a hotspot for graffiti artists to (legally) do their thing.

Royal Festival Hall

DO

Take in some culture, of course. As well as the **Southbank Centre** arts complex, this part of town is home to the **Old Vic**, **Young Vic** and **National Theatre**, two **BFI** cinemas, the **Rambert** dance company, **The Vaults** alternative theatre space and the **Florence Nightingale Museum**.

EAT

For a bargain pre- or post-show dinner, it's hard to beat **Maries**, a tiny BYOB Thai-British cafe on Lower Marsh. There's a branch of popular Malaysian street-food spot **Roti King** nearby too, while **Mamuśka** serves great-value pierogi (and vodka shots) in the Leake Street arches. By the river, you'll find **La Gamba**, a seafood specialist delivering Spanish holiday vibes, and the excellent National Theatre outpost of Peckham favourite **Forza Wine**.

DRINK

Lower Marsh is an underrated go-to, whether you're after coffee at art cafe **The Glitch** or day-and-night hangout **Scooter Caffe**, a pint at theatrical pub **Vaulty Towers** or mojitos at **Cubana**.

SHOP

Lower Marsh is also home to a clutch of indie shops, including **Greensmiths** grocery, giftshop **Twice the Siren** and even fetishware emporium **Honour** – plus a variety of market stalls from Monday to Saturday. Also pop by **The Calder**, a bookshop with a tiny theatre on The Cut – and of course, the daily **South Bank Book Market** under Waterloo Bridge.

Above: Royal Festival Hall
Below: South Bank Book Market; Forza Wine

BFI SOUTHBANK

BFI Southbank

39

DEPTFORD & NEW CROSS

Art-school cool meets inner-city grit

It's been over 20 years since people started describing Deptford and New Cross as 'up-and-coming', and yet they remain more low-key than neighbouring Peckham (no.37). Deptford was a shipbuilding hub for centuries, and the area still has a few nautical flourishes, like the metal anchor on its High Street and the Royal Naval School building – now home to Goldsmiths art college, cradle of many an indie band. Heavy Luftwaffe bombing and post-war rebuilding have left their mark; more recently, immigration and patchy gentrification have shaped the vibe. The arches around Deptford station (the longest-serving railway station in London, fact fans) have been revamped into a cobbled 'village' called Deptford Market Yard and the post-industrial space at Convoys Wharf is awaiting thousands of new riverside flats. Dramatic change could still be on its way. But for now, Deptford and New Cross feel like just the right balance of grit and gems.

Deptford Market Yard

<u>DO</u>

Explore the cultural goings-on at **Goldsmiths Centre for Contemporary Art,** long-serving arts centre **The Albany,** and the **Trinity Laban** dance theatre – plus gigs at the **New Cross Inn** and **Piehouse Co-Op**, occasional performances at the 18th-century **Master Shipwright's House** on the Thames and makers' fairs at the **Cockpit** studios.

<u>EAT</u>

There's a great range of food here, from upmarket Italian at **Marcella** and Japanese at **Kekaki Izakaya**, right through to affordable Vietnamese at **Moc** and Chinese at **Uncle Wrinkle**. Don't miss seasonal wine bar **Klose & Soan** for a laid-back treat dinner.

<u>DRINK</u>

The Dog & Bell isn't just Deptford's best pub, it's one of London's finest: a cosy community haven with live folk and jazz sessions and an annual Pickle Festival. Elsewhere, you'll find craft beers at **Villages**, natty wines at **ZÉ-ZÉ** and kitsch cocktails in an eye-popping setting at both branches of **Little Nan's**.

<u>SHOP</u>

Deptford Market is a must: it's one of London's most eclectic street markets, with groceries and household goods alongside what you might charitably call bric-a-brac. You can also pick up vinyl at **Upside Down Records** and **Planet Wax**, books at **The Word Bookshop** and **Zennoni**, vintage at **Rag N Bone** and bargain antiques at **Second Time Around**.

Above: Trinity Laban; The Dog & Bell
Below: Deptford Market; Goldsmiths, University of London

40

LONDON BRIDGE & SOUTHWARK

Food and culture by the bank of the Thames

For centuries, Southwark was London's naughty little sister: a separate settlement south of the Thames, known for licentious fun (bear-baiting, sex work, theatre). Chaucer started his *Canterbury Tales* at Southwark's Tabard Inn; Shakespeare built his original Globe here; young Charles Dickens lived here while his dad was locked up in a prison on today's Borough High Street. London Bridge station has been running constantly since 1836; Guy's Hospital dates back to 1721; and Borough Market has been trading for over a thousand years. There are newcomers too: the gargantuan Bankside Power Station, now housing Tate Modern; the Millennium Bridge, known by Londoners as 'the Wobbly Bridge' for the way it swayed unnervingly when first opened; and of course, London's tallest building, The Shard. Dotted among the landmarks are historic streets, with top dining and drinking options tucked away amid offices and railway viaducts.

Borough Market

DO

See an exhibition (or wander the free permanent collection) at **Tate Modern** or a play at **Shakespeare's Globe** – or at the more experimental **Menier Chocolate Factory**. **Omeara** hosts intimate gigs in a splendid ballroom space. You can also ogle vintage surgical implements at the **Old Operating Theatre Museum**, explore pan-African culture at **The Africa Centre** or pay tribute to London's unnamed dead at the **Crossbones Graveyard** memorial.

EAT

Don't fancy street food? Borough Market and the nearby arches are lined with sit-down restaurants, including pasta specialists **Padella**, Spanish importers **Brindisa**, Thai favourite **Kolae** and Sri Lankan hotspot **Rambutan**. Or settle in for a fry-up at greasy spoon **Terry's**.

DRINK

For a pint with some history, duck into **The George**, London's last galleried coaching inn, dating back to the 1670s. Pop over the road for cocktails at **Swift**, catch an acoustic set with your beer at **The Gladstone Arms** or split the G at **Mc & Sons**. If all you want is coffee, **Scenery** will see you right.

SHOP

Borough Market – one of London's oldest food markets – is a gourmand's dream, with stalls selling everything from deli meats to fruit and veg. (Arrive early on a weekday to dodge the crowds.) Nearby **Borough Kitchen** is the place to go for your next kitchen gadget.

Padella

ART CHANGES WE CHANGE

Above: Roupell Street
Opposite: Tate Modern

IMAGE CREDITS

Image credits in order of appearance (left to right): © Mark Phillips; © Mark Phillips, © The Royal Parks; Soho: © Jon Ingall, © Ianni Dimitrov, © Jansos, © Leslie Lau; Covent Garden: © Haley Green, © Mike in London, © Alex Serge; China Town: © FotoVoyager, © Ilyas Ayub; The City: © Taran Wilkhu, © JE Whyte, © Rachael Smith, © Mauritius Images GmbH; Bloomsbury:© David Post, © Taran Wilkhu, © Milly Kenny-Ryder, © Ellen Christina Hancock, © Coward Lion; Clerkenwell: © Ian Crowson, © Adam Slama, © Taran Wilkhu, © Beth Evans, © Sam A. Harris, © Simon Turner; Mayfair and St James's: © Helen Cathcart, © Samuel Regan Asante, © Andres GarciaM, © Alex de Corte Install view "Helter Shelter or: The Red Show! Or…", 2021. Sadie Coles. Photo Eva Herzog, © Helen Cathcart; Marylebone: © Francesca Grima, © David Post, © SMP News, © Chanel Irvine, © Chanel Irvine; Kensington: © Andy Paradis / Royal Albert Hall, © Peter Kelleher, © Dirk Linder, © Shruti Veeramachineni Gravity Road, © Mike Clegg; Notting Hill: © Anthony Bressy, © The Pelican, © Ellen Christina Hancock, © Fineas Anton, © Lesley Lau, © Tony Farrugia; Chelsea: © Simon Turner, © Sam Bush, © Ellen Christina Hancock, © Chanel Irvine, © Matt Chung / Saatchi Gallery; Queen's Park: © Mickey Lee, © Milly Kenny-Ryder; Chiswick: © Michael Jones, © Ian Dagnall, © Chanel Irvine, © Isabell Hernandez; Richmond: © Marco Kessler, © Petersham Nurseries; Stoke Newington: © ZoneTwoandBeyond, © Richard Barnes, © Chanel Irvine, © Lesley Lau, © David Post, © Richard Newstead; Camden Town: © Jim Monk, © Roberto Herrett, © JGGFCP, © Chanel Irvine, © Ian Macpherson; Crouch End: © Marco Kessler, © Beam, © Ellen Christina Hancock, © David Post, © David Post; King's Cross: © Simon Hart, © Lesley Lau, © Taran Wilkhu; Tottenham: © Edward Hill courtesy OOF Gallery, © Tom Carter, © Pressure Drop Taproom, © With Milk London, © Brian Dandridge; Highbury: © Pat Tuson, © PA Images, © Milly Kenny-Ryder, © Ellen Christina Hancock, © David Post; Hampstead: © David Jacobs, © Greg Balfour Evans, © Marco Kessler, © Alla Tsyganova, © Magdalena Bujak, © Marco Kessler, © Marco Kessler, © Jack Calverley; Bow & Victoria Park Village: © Martin Usborne, © David Post, © David Post, © Virginia Malavasi, © Colours of Arley; Stratford: © Marco Kessler, © Hufton + Crow, © Jonathan Perugia; Shoreditch & Spitalfields © Yoav Aziz, © Charlotte Schreiber, © Chanel Irvine, © Ollie Singleton, © Maartje Hensen, © Robert Evans; London Fields: © Chanel Irvine, © Madeline Waller, © Ola Smit, © Chanel Irvine, © Martin Usborne, © Charlotte Schreiber; Dalston: © Chanel Irvine, © Beth Davis, © Helen Cathcart, © Milly Kenny-Ryder, © Charlotte Schreiber, © Taran Wilkhu; Bethnal Green: © Alena Kravchenko, © Harriet Langford, © Charlotte Schreiber, © Gleren Meneghin, © Gulja Holland, © Chanel Irvine; Leyton & Leytonstone: © Nathaniel Noir, © David Post; Lower Clapton, © Chanel Irvine, © Ellen Christina Hancock, © Orlando Gilli, © Charlotte Schreiber; Walthamstow: © Roger Garfield, © Daniel Shearing, © Monica Wells, © David Levene, © Chanel Irvine, © Adam Isfendiyar; Battersea: © Eduard Pretsi, © Marco Kessler; Vauxhall: © Ianni Dimitrov, © Alex Macleod; Dulwich & Herne Hill: © Sebastien Mercier, © Taran Wilkhu, © Lulu's, © Lesley Lau, © Tony French, © Martin Usborne; Greenwich: © Benedek , © Chris Dorney, © Old Royal Naval College; Brixton: ©SMP News, © Angela Hampton, © David Post, © Jennifer Cauli / Three Uncles, © Ellen Christina Hancock; Bermondsey: © Chanel Irvine, © David Post, © Chanel Irvine, © Trent McMinn, © Chanel Irvine; Peckham: ©Simon Whybray, hi boo i love you., 2016 © Deniz Guzel, courtesy Bold Tendencies, © Rhea Dillon, 9_3 or I know how to fall (3) and I was born to nights (9)(2022) © Bold Tendencies 2022. Photography by Deniz Guzel, © David Post, © Sam A. Harris, © Simon Turner, © Bold Tendencies, courtesy Bold Tendencies, © Yuki Sugiura; Waterloo & The South Bank: ©Ianni Dimitrov Pictures, © Gregory Wrona, © Chanel Irvine, © Sam A Harris, © Luke Hayes / BFI; Deptford & New Cross: © Image Source Limited, © Taran Wilkhu, © Horst Friedrichs, © Chanel Irvine, © Taran Wilkhu; London Bridge & Southwark: © Chanel Irvine, © Padella, © Taran Wilkhu, © Mickey Lee.

An Opinionated Guide to London Neighbourhoods
First edition, first printing

Published in 2026 by Hoxton Mini Press, London.
Copyright © Hoxton Mini Press 2026. All rights reserved.

Text by James Manning
Editing by Florence Ward
Production design by Dom Grant
Production control by David Brimble
Proofreading by Dean Drake
Editorial support by Richard Enright

With thanks to Matthew Young for
initial series design.

Please note: we recommend checking the
websites of featured locations and
businesses before you visit for the latest
information on price, opening times and
pre-booking requirements.

Thank you to all of the individuals and
institutions who have provided images
and arranged permissions. While every
effort has been made to trace the present
copyright holders we apologise in advance
for any unintentional omission or error,
and would be pleased to insert the
appropriate acknowledgement in any
subsequent edition.

A CIP catalogue record for this book is
available from the British Library.

ISBN: 978-1-917719-00-1

Printed and bound by OZGraf, Poland

Manufacturer: Hoxton Mini Press, 104
Northside Studios, 16–29 Andrews Road,
London E8 4QF, UK
www.hoxtonminipress.com

Represented by: Authorised Rep
Compliance Ltd., Ground Floor, 71 Lower
Baggot Street, Dublin DO2 P593, Ireland
www.arccompliance.com

Hoxton Mini Press is an environmen-
tally conscious publisher, committed
to offsetting our carbon footprint.
This book is 100 per cent carbon
compensated, with offset purchased
from Stand For Trees.

Every time you order from our website, we
plant a tree: www.hoxtonminipress.com

Selected opinionated guides in the series:

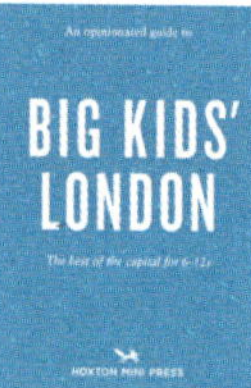

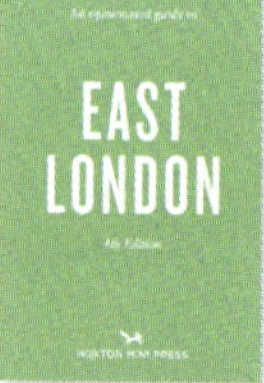

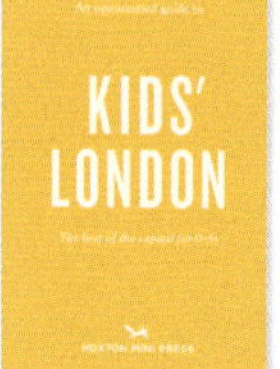

For more go to www.hoxtonminipress.com

INDEX